Who the F*ck do you THINK you are?

Who the F*ck do you THINK you are?

THE ULTIMATE GUIDE: EMPOWERING YOU TO LEARN WHO YOU ARE, BE CONFIDENT AND DISCOVER HOW TO BE YOUR TRUE SELF

Geri Carey

authors
AND CO.

First published in Great Britain in 2024
by Authors & Co.
www.authorsandco.pub

ISBN 978-1-915771-71-1 (paperback)

Disclaimer

This book is intended to be a helpful guide on the topics discussed. It is not written as a diagnostic tool or a treatment for any condition. Please be sure to consult a medical practitioner before you make any decisions that may affect your health.

This book is firstly dedicated to my children, a gentle reminder to stay true to yourself, your authenticity and instinct will guide you along the way. Don't be afraid to shine bright and celebrate yourself, unapologetically lean into the things that light you up, remember in any given moment, when you change what you think about yourself you can change your entire life.

Secondly my soul mate David, it was you that showed me just how much a person can grow and flourish in the right conditions. Thank you for seeing me when I didn't want to be seen and always trusting me to find the way back to myself, I am forever grateful.

Contents

Introduction

Thank you for choosing this book, I am so happy you are here, I cannot wait for you to find out who you think you are, change what you think about yourself and help you to become the leader of your own life.

Who you **THINK** you are is central to everything in your life, it's the part of your mind that decides pretty much everything from your beliefs, decisions, actions and relationships they are all guided by the person you think you are. This thinking affects the way you interact with the world around you and most importantly it controls the hidden world inside you. Those personal inside thoughts that influence who you think are also shape your identity, which is as unique as your fingerprint. Often these deep-rooted beliefs are hidden and thinking just happens, which can be a problem especially if they are negative and unhelpful. We are not generally taught or shown how to connect with ourselves or question our beliefs on a deeper level and so we often navigate life as we are in that very moment. If you're not aware of what thinking is going on behind the scenes then you may find yourself stuck, not feel connected to yourself or asking yourself who am I?

Identity Crisis?

Some years ago, I started to notice a lot of people were struggling to connect with their identities and would mention they didn't know who they were, they felt anxious, lost or stuck. I deeply recognised those same feelings I had experienced a few years ago, not feeling happy, confused, anxious, yet a strong desire to grow. Most, like me, had a crisis of identity following a big life experience such as having a child, changing career, ending relationships, or losing loved ones. All of us had the same thing in common: a disconnection from ourselves as the person we thought we were and a yearning to become something more.

Finding myself

As the years went by and the more I connected with my true self, I noticed the relationship with myself and others began to change for the better. The conversations became deeper; people seemed to talk to me more freely and would tell me they felt a sense of safety. The unspoken authenticity that was now a part of me seemed to be interesting and refreshing to people, and I noticed often, when I spoke about my real feelings, set boundaries, or shared my honest thoughts, people would literally sigh in relief as I subconsciously encouraged them to do the same. This incredible self-awareness helped me to build the connection to my true self, I was then able to explore the burning curiosity about learning more about who I was. In this new awareness, I leaned into the parts of me that felt authentic, and through trusting myself, I had the ability to look beyond my circumstances, changing what I thought about myself, I changed my life.

I have experienced first-hand that how you think about yourself creates the person you are and this thinking designs a set of unique guidelines you will follow for life. It will choose the person in the driving seat who will help you or stop you from achieving all the fantastic things you are capable of. We all have a right to live our life on our terms, It's pretty important you get to know exactly what lies beneath your everyday actions and decisions because these are the foundations that have created your unique identity.

What about you?

Perhaps you don't know who you are right now and can't move forward, or you know exactly the type of person you need to become and have taken action, and still, you're not getting anywhere. You may need to turn your attention inward to help you uncover who you are and find any hidden reasons behind the actions you take or don't take. It could be the perfect time for a self-check-in. Discovering your True Self is the first step to creating a more fulfilled life.

This book will help you delve into the beliefs you hold about yourself—beliefs that may have disguised your true self. I will share the tools and wisdom I used to help navigate you towards your authentic self—a self uniquely designed by you, for you. I want to help you uncover what makes you the person you THINK you are. I encourage you throughout the book to become self-led, the leader of your life and your thinking. You will learn the self-awareness to build your very own steady foundations that will support you in achieving long lasting success. The reality is the life decisions you have made so far such as applying for a new job, starting or ending relationships, financial investments and so on have all been guided by the person you think you are. As you learn to lead a Self-Led Life®, you will know what thoughts from the inside are being used to help guide YOUR life on the outside. You will be able to use your new self-awareness to inform your everyday choices using the tools and resources to help yourself and others along the way. This book will help you meet your true self; through insights and inspired actions, you will learn radical self-awareness and dig out any hidden thoughts or beliefs that are getting in your way.

We're in this together

I will be with you every step of the way sharing lightbulb moments that will help you to uncover your own insights that will help you to illuminate a new way of thinking. Life is precious and full of twists and turns, and it's meant for you to fully experience it all as the person you were meant to be. It's never too late to unlearn all the thinking that has led you to question who you really are. Quite often, as you catapult through life at a million miles an hour, you don't get a chance to think about who you are, and like me you may find yourself asking the big questions when the pace of your life changes or after experiencing a big life event.

It can be hard to find a moment to really think about who you are when life is busy. Life just seems to happen; you tend to deal with things only when there's an issue or challenge as time whizzes by. But it doesn't have to be that way, I think everyone should have easy access to resources and insightful information that helps them to live a life that is guided by them.

Do we have a choice?

I believed that my personality developed naturally over time. I thought that as we age, our experiences teach us more and that's how we mature. Until I hit the point of feeling that I wasn't sure who I was, I felt lost and disconnected. After experiencing my big moment; breakdown, burnout whatever you want to call it, I was lost in 'no man's land'. I felt empty, I wasn't feeling connected to the person I was anymore, and I didn't want to 'get back to my old self' as per the standard message we often hear. I wanted something else, but I wasn't sure how to get there or what the heck it was. Leaning into this curiosity and holding on for dear life, I dedicated years of searching to find out precisely who I was and who was on the other side of the uneasy feeling. I needed to find the Geri behind the labels, conditions and beliefs. So I grabbed the big jigsaw puzzle that was my life as I knew it and threw it up in the air into what felt like a million pieces. Slowly but surely, over the years, I began to put the puzzle back together whilst carefully selecting only the pieces that I chose, the little precious pieces of me that were seen, understood, loved and accepted by me. Being able to lead myself, I realised I didn't need all of the pieces to complete my puzzle; I just needed to choose the ones I liked, and in the end, it turned out to be perfect.

Self-awareness is the key

My journey required a lot of major self-awareness, it was radical, and it was not straightforward, but my goodness, it was incredible. In training to be a therapist, I was so fortunate to access the most astonishing academic theory and training. Learning about relating to others helped me to deeply relate to myself and reflect on my own life and experiences. Each lecture, essay, and new person I met all provided me with little clues and hunches that I followed; they led me to places within myself that I didn't know were there. The permission I needed to start looking at myself closely had been given; how could I expect to help others to find themselves if I hadn't found me? The thought of helping others gave me the courage to look at myself. The amazing thing about person-centred practice is the magic of the space and therapeutic relationship that allows you to explore your inner world. Through years of studying and practicing self-reflection and awareness, I have been able to rethink and rewrite my reality and design a future connected to the person I know I am today. I am no longer driven by outdated beliefs or responses to trauma, I am aligned with my authentic self. It feels like I have a warm, safe place inside that gently guides me and gives me the confidence to live as myself. These days, when I face obstacles, I can face them myself with clarity and confidence. Being able to choose those puzzle pieces has given me a chance to reset and live life on my terms, a life where my inside matches the outside. I believe that we all have the right to be able to choose who we are and how we show up in the world but also to know what reasons sit behind some of the challenges or discomfort we are feeling.

This book and companion share my personal lightbulb moments, and inspired actions to help guide you on your journey. This isn't a typical self-help book, nor is it a replacement for therapy, it's about gaining new knowledge and a powerful sense of awareness that will help you lead your own life.

My mission is to help thousands of people worldwide access the safe space they already have within them and guide themselves through life with radical awareness and compassion.

To help you lead a Self-Led Life®, I combine coaching and concepts from counselling, psychology, and psychotherapy, all of which will guide you along the way of self-discovery.

My aim is that during our time together you will uncover your true values, meaning and purpose to be empowered to challenge your thinking. You will be able to manage the challenges you face such as feeling lost, unfulfilled or disconnected. Throughout this book your new insights and inspired actions will help you to build your own foundations and a toolkit that will help you to lead a Self-Led Life®.

Being able to lead yourself and understand your unique identity, will springboard you into designing a future that resonates with your true self – the person you know you are. Most of all, you will create a huge tidal wave, not a ripple; who wants that? Go big or go home. With a new level of self-awareness and knowledge, you will become a cycle breaker, change maker and unapologetically yourself.

Throughout the book I will be guiding you through the 8 Pillars of a Self-Led Life®.

1. Self-knowledge: Understanding who you are at your core and your ability to think about your aspirational self.
2. Self-Beliefs: The perceptions you hold about your capabilities and worth.
3. How it started: How your culture and environment have shaped your perspective.
4. Unseen influences: The unspoken rules and conditions you are living by.
5. Interaction with the world: Your ability to empathise and connect and your emotional intelligence.
6. Self-compassion: Treating yourself with kindness and understanding.

7. Authenticity: Current level of authenticity, feelings of congruence/incongruence.
8. Purpose-driven goals & values: that are informed by your thoughts.

Take the first step in radical self-awareness and discover how self-led you are. Head to **gericarey.com** and take the Self-Led Life quiz® where you will get instant results and a personalised report.

The person at the centre

Learning about person-centred theory was life-changing, the amazing Carl Rogers' humanistic approach was what helped me to first understand myself and humans in a way I find hard to describe. Which I appreciate isn't very useful for a book! I recall almost instantly after picking up his book 'On Becoming a Person', feeling emotions stronger than any words, the main one was a deep sense of relief as I suddenly felt a sense of what I can only describe as acceptance. I also discovered there was meaning behind some deep-rooted feelings of anger, abandonment, and unworthiness. My first lightbulb moment happened when I learned that Rogers believed all humans have an in-built desire to thrive despite our circumstances.

This theory he calls The Actualizing Tendency excited me to learn more about human flourishing because if that was the case, then what is stopping us all from reaching 'Our full potential'? Why did I and so many other people struggle to reach this 'thing'?

I leaned into the curiosity of finding out more about why we humans struggle to reach our full potential and the identity crisis I and others have experienced. I concluded that, for me, the two things were somehow related, how could we reach our potential if we didn't know or weren't connected to our true selves?

Research Eureka moment!

During my time at University, I completed a self-study on how I cultivated my own authenticity. I decided to take a deep dive into my authenticity to help me both grow as a person and as a therapist. This type of research meant self-awareness was needed by the bucket loads, I thought I already knew who I was and found more than I could have imagined.

Hats off to my husband, children and friends they watched in surprise as I stepped away from the world as I knew it, not only had I decided to start university as a very mature student I was now studying myself. I spent most days in a very simple way, walking alone wearing no makeup dressed in comfy walking clothes, observing everything as I slowed down the pace of my life. It lasted for months. The first step I had to write down was all my day-to-day experiences, everyday encounters with people, hunches, and thoughts, every single day, this was classed as my data.

Can you imagine? The information I collected consisted of photos I had taken on walks, dreams, diary extracts, voice notes, and even capturing emotions after conversations with people. Looking back, I really do laugh at what people must have thought of me during this time.

The next stage was pulling all the information together, my office looked like a police investigation wall full of photos, post it notes, pins and arrows.

It was during the process of looking for themes and pulling it all together, I started to spot some interesting things followed by what is known as a *eureka* moment. I realised the person I was couldn't help me create a better life. As I followed hunches and paid attention to what lit me up, I also recognised the crippling self-doubt and anxiety I was living with. I faced myself head on as I questioned relationships, and I discovered just how much I was holding myself back. I needed to understand the deep routed and outdated beliefs that I had grown to accept as truth because it became clear they were no longer helping me.

'You can't really know where you're going, unless you know where you have been.'

— Maya Angelou

I remember when I felt disconnected from my identity; I desperately wanted to find a way home, but I had no clue how to get there. Finally, through research and radical awareness, I was able to lead myself to my true self; I became the expert of me, my own best friend and cheerleader, and in the process, I realised I had designed a new way of living and thinking, the Self-Led Life®.

Being self-led isn't a substitute for therapy, it is about knowing who you truly are and what is in the foundations you have supporting you. This next level of awareness provides you with knowledge of how to build a solid set of foundations that will help you to have a plan and structure to support your future goals and aspirations. You are the star of this book, my job here is to support you and bring my experiences and the fascinating theories together to show you how you can lead a life that is yours, created by you for you. If, like me, you have identified a gap between who you are and who you want to be, and you are prepared to take inspired action to get there, then this truly is the book for you.

If you're feeling anxious try to see this opportunity to learn together as a blessing, some people truly believe they don't have the power to change. They will accept that life happens, and they are dictated by the actions and beliefs of the outside world. I promise having the ability to tune into yourself will change your life.

I believe you can do this, be an unapologetic cycle breaker and be the person you are meant to be, you can lean into the desire to reach your full potential and create the life you deserve.

This book is not an invitation for you to scrutinise the past but rather, a gentle nudge for you to explore some of the beliefs that have shaped you into who you think you are today. Ultimately, you will decide if these beliefs are a part of who you are, if they will help you to lean into your full potential, or if they are holding you back.

Before we start, can I ask you to think about why you want to know who you are and why you want to lead a Self-Led Life®?

Think about your real why and answer five times!

WHY five times? Because your real why often sits below the surface of what you think is your why, so you have to do some digging.

Here's an example of mine, WHY do you want to learn about yourself?' *To stop feeling anxious, out of sorts.*'

WHY? So I can feel better
WHY? To stop feeling so unworthy
WHY? Because I need to have my own back
WHY? Because I am stopping myself from following my heart and life is too short.

When you have your real reason, write it on the next page, it will give you that little extra nudge serving as a reminder every time you open the book.

This book is going to take some work on your behalf, the good news is you can go at your own pace and there are plenty of resources on the website to help you. I want to empower you to find the resources you already have within you and be able to navigate the world confidently. In this awareness, you will make decisions driven by you, how you present yourself will be more considered, and relationships and confidence will improve.

To help you get the most out of this book and to help you get to grips with the theory, I recommend that you use the FREE book companion provided visit **gericarey.com**. Inside there's lots of space to note your insights, build your toolkit and it's a powerful keepsake to use for life. Good luck on this adventure, I am with you every step of the way.

What is your real why, what's important to you and why do you want to find out more about who you really are?

My Owl

One of the most fascinating things born from my research project on authenticity was discovering my 'Inner Owl'. As part of the research process, I had to make time to practise self-reflection and then capture every experience I had. When I first learned about research, I thought I would be interviewing people and analysing statistics, I never imagined there was such a process that would facilitate such a profound journey of self-exploration. What a lightbulb that was, there is an actual process for researching my own human experience.

Having a reason to regularly take notes and keep a diary worked perfectly for me as I have always dipped in and out of journaling, feeling I never quite got it right. I have always dabbled over the years but quite frankly I wouldn't have wanted anyone to find anything I had written; I felt vulnerable writing, if the words came out, they were real. Looking at it as a project and having to capture this 'data' as part of the research made it feel exciting.

The research findings were incredible; buried under all that data, I found something magical. In the masses of information I had gathered, I spotted a steady warm force within me that constantly pushed me forward; like an inner knowing, mixed with an instinct to thrive, I had discovered a new part of me that made it *safe to dream*.

It became so significant that I named it my **Wise Owl.**

This incredible force guided me as I navigated the tender journey of looking into my past; it held my hand as I questioned and dared to explore the meaning of some relationships and helped me uncover my purpose. The research helped me to understand my identity on another level and had such an impact on me that I became obsessed with the idea of sharing what I discovered to help others. It never ended, and it flows into the pages of this book.

I wanted to find a way of easily sharing the mountains of academic information to help people to better understand themselves and lead their own lives.

I do this in an easy-to-understand and straightforward way, be prepared for some work though, this book is bursting with information and practical exercises. I hope in reading this book and using the resources that you find your hidden Owl and your safe place, and you lead yourself with confidence and worthiness on the many adventures that lie ahead for you.

Cracking open

Cracked open, just like a seed, you must crack open before you grow. It feels like the end of something, it's the unknown and feels lonely and raw, but as I have experienced from this place, it's possible to grow. Some people will experience 'cracking open' in many different ways; perhaps a breakdown, identity crisis, or rock bottom, it's the moment when you have no more to give and you're fed up with feeling fed up. I felt like a stranger in my own body, I was overweight, terrified, ashamed, frightened, tired, exhausted, and depressed. I felt overwhelmingly responsible for what felt like the world; my 'situation' was described by the doctor and others as burnout, but on reflection, I was also 'burned in'. From the outside it was clear to see I was broken, but only I could feel the chaos that I was managing on the inside.

Throughout my life, until my mid-thirties, I kept myself so busy managing the symptoms of anxiety it became a normal part of my daily routine. I had a job, family, and other commitments, I had no choice, I couldn't afford to slow down. Everyone's cracking open moment is different, and if my experience is anything to go by, it doesn't always stop you in your tracks. It can go on for years undetected as you subconsciously jump from one symptom or sign to the next, fixing it as you go.

My last 'cracked open moment' happened several years ago, after I had long ignored my body's many warning signs telling me to stop and pause. I was suffering from crippling anxiety and unknown unprocessed trauma. I was papering over the cracks and ignoring my body's cries for help until it was no longer an option; Distracting myself on the outside wasn't working, I had start looking at what was going on from the inside.

Who's making these decisions?

I don't think anyone saw it coming. I have created many disguises over my life, imaginary fronts that helped me to navigate the world safely every day. They all had the same job, to tell the outside world I was okay, happy, and successful. I struggled to continue to hide behind them as my outside world changed; excessive weight gain, skin conditions, panic disorder, and health anxiety were all well and truly on show. Something deeper was happening to me inside, and I had no idea of how to handle it or what it was. In my desperate search for answers and change I juiced, I fasted, tried yoga, joined a women's circle, read books, loaned a horse, bought a cleaning business, manufactured friendships, and spent thousands of pounds on self-development, gym equipment and retreats. I was managing to build some self-confidence as I did the 'things' that I thought would help, but I still felt there was something missing. On reflection, most of these choices were fuelled by my lack of self-worth, but at the time, I wasn't aware of the reasons behind my decisions. I remember constantly feeling lost and detached. I couldn't connect to my identity. Who I wanted to be felt unreachable; my inside didn't match my outside.

I had enough and was exhausted, I realised I needed to look inside and learn the reasons behind my actions and what was truly holding me back. I know I was doing the best I could in the circumstances I was facing, but I didn't have the self-awareness at the time to understand the wider impact of my actions. Although I thought I was strong at the time, looking back, the decisions I made were only temporary fixes, but they ended up impacting my mental health and worsened my terrible relationship with money. Each time I failed to find this so-called happiness, it would result in more self-doubt and anxiety, I was stuck and I needed to find out who I was.

I missed the memo

I couldn't be present with my children. I was so preoccupied with thinking I was going to get poorly that I would constantly be in a state of anxiety. Almost every conversation I had with my husband would be about the latest ailment I had; what I thought it was, how bad it could be, and yet I was too worried to make a doctor's appointment and carried on putting on weight.

I was on a million-mile-an-hour roller coaster, constantly managing the symptoms of weight gain, hair loss, irritable bowel disease, heart palpitations, panic disorder, psoriasis, stomach ache, blurred vision, vertigo, indigestion and GURD. In between school runs and trying to work I would spend hours in bed, I would always gravitate back to this warm space, almost like a baby. My IBS became so chronic that I was regularly caught short walking back from the school drop-off, and it was only a 10-minute walk. When I would shower, I would imagine it was the day I would find a lump, my blood would run cold as I imagined the scenario. In the night, I would dream that I was being given a terminal diagnosis, and my family was laughing at me, one night, my panic was so bad that I woke up after a nightmare and was frantically gasping for air and fainted. All of these things were trying to tell me something, my body was screaming at me, enough is enough.

Experiencing physical symptoms due to unresolved trauma and PTSD and hiding within yourself is a very real response. If you haven't read The Body Keeps the Score, I highly recommend it - it's a fantastic explanation of how we can experience illness due to our internal mental state and this was undoubtedly the truth for me, this book helped me to further look inwards.

While you're at it...

To be honest I think I've always been a little 'cracked open' and I think it's a place I could return to as I navigate life but with my new awareness, I will be able to handle it better. When I was at my lowest point, I think my mind took the opportunity to get rid of the other big stuff that I needed to deal with, 'while you're at it, let's look at these bits that were hidden,' and Boom! It happened they all came at once; all the buried things that sat piling up in the background, like my parents' and nephews' death, court cases, toxic relationships and finally when my sister died - Boom. Trying to be a mum, wife, and business owner (the job I thought I wanted), it is no wonder I felt like I was failing at it all.

I headed to therapy, and I want to be honest here; I found it hard at first. I was embarrassed and ashamed, but I went out of pure desperation. It took time but it helped, what I find amazing about therapy is it's not just about what happens in the room, it's also about the moments of illumination you get in between sessions. Over time I found myself getting braver and braver in exploring my world, my internal power was getting stronger each day. I was starting to give myself some quality nourishment, starting with the journey of being aware of my feelings, and now it was about having the courage to be curious.

I know first-hand that we can busy ourselves as a way of dealing with trauma. I would say it's almost THE way, and it certainly worked for most of my life.

In the rare moments of stillness when I was alone, I would feel terror. Therapy was different, having someone see me and listen non-judgementally with compassion, enabled me to explore my feelings. One day, during a session, out of nowhere, I felt the strong urge to want to reflect on my younger years. The floodgates had opened, and I felt what can only be described as an overwhelming feeling of being unloveable in my rawness. Wow, if this feeling was what was sitting in the background, then no wonder I felt like shit!

I wanted to peek under the bonnet and look at my past, I knew the sense of worthlessness was holding me back, it felt heavy. It is a deeply personal decision to choose to explore your past, as often it can be painful and raw. It can be typical to want to make sense of past experiences, our brain also likes to make connections. Looking at the route of the thoughts enabled me to make sense of some of the unhelpful thinking that I was trapped in but it's not necessary for everyone. You may choose not to look at your past, and that's fine, everyone's journey is different. We are all unique, being self-led here means following your judgement, treating yourself with kindness and seeking help if you need it.

My worth in their hands

It is recognised that the love and acceptance you receive from your parents or caregivers will generally set the benchmark for your self-worth. The UK Government developed **The best start for life**: a vision for the 1,001 critical days as part of the early year's healthy development review. This time frame is critical because it lays the foundation for a person's emotional and physical health, brain development, and ability to form relationships throughout their life. Here's a simple explanation of why it shows we need to be more aware of our own early years' experience:

Brain Development: In the first 1001 days of life, a baby's brain grows faster than at any other time. During this period, the experiences and environment a child is exposed to can significantly influence the brain's development. Positive experiences, like love, care, and stimulation, can encourage healthy brain development. On the other hand, negative experiences, like neglect or stress, can harm it.

Emotional Health: The early years are crucial for developing emotional health. How we are treated and how our needs are met in these early days can shape our ability to manage emotions, cope with stress, and relate to others as we grow up.

Physical Health: Early nutrition, healthcare, and physical care are essential for preventing diseases and conditions later in life. Good health in the early years helps set the stage for physical well-being throughout life.

Attachment and Relationships: The relationships and bonds formed in the early days, particularly with parents and caregivers, are foundational for how we form relationships in the future. Secure attachments lead to better outcomes in terms of social skills, education, and emotional health.

Life-long Impact: The experiences and care received during these 1001 days can have a lasting impact on an individual's life. They can influence education, employment, mental health, and even the ability to parent in the future.

> "Science tells us that a child's experiences from conception through their first five years will go on to shape their next 50. It tells us that the kind of children we raise today, will reflect the kind of world we will live in tomorrow. It tells us that investing in the start of life is not an indulgence, but economically, socially and psychologically vital to a prosperous society."
>
> — Jason Knauf, CEO of the Royal Foundation, December 2020

By understanding the importance of our own early years, we can appreciate the significant impact this period has on our life. When I started to think about my start in life, the penny finally dropped. How could I love myself when I didn't get what I needed as a child? When what you need just isn't available from the people who bring you into this world, then I believe it can create negative beliefs that you hold about yourself, in my case, I felt unlovable. How you are loved or not in your early years sets the tone for how you will feel about yourself.

Understanding the environment in which you were raised and the connection you had with your parents or caregivers when you were younger may help explain some of the reasons for the challenges you are facing today, such as low confidence, self-esteem, etc. This isn't an invitation for you to seek conflict, it's about practising self-compassion and empathy. There may be some reasons when you look back with compassion you can see your parents or caregivers did the best they could do in the circumstances they were in. Or you may have parent(s) or caregivers who helped you to pick up some fantastic beliefs you hold about yourself. But I also need to mention the people who may be in my situation which is, no matter what amount of soul-searching I do there will never be a reason to accept or understand some of the choices your parents made.

And that's ok; again, nothing is 'normal'. We're all experiencing this thing called life as individuals.

Research suggests being raised by an emotionally unavailable parent or guardian can lead to unstable friendships, failed relationships, emotional distress, an inability to self-regulate and provide for yourself, and identity confusion.

If you have been deprived of emotional needs in early childhood, it's known as developmental trauma, which can lead to long-term effects if not adequately addressed. I wanted to share this with you as it helped me explain the reasons for the challenges we sometimes face as adults. When I learned that how I was loved would affect me, I could treat myself with more self-compassion. I could see how the thoughts I held about myself led to some poor decisions, it all made sense. Through lots of self-acceptance and self-love, I can now provide myself with the validation I need. Your self-worth can be updated at any time, it's not based on your parent's love and acceptance. You can see any negative thoughts as a chance to get closer to yourself - it sounds cheesy, but you really can love yourself more than anyone else in the world. It's good to recognise where any feelings of low self-esteem may have come from.

Being self-led means that you choose to prioritise loving yourself and this can kick in when any feelings such as unworthiness start to surface. If this section has prompted you to want to learn more, make a note on your reading list, there is a lot of excellent research, and if you feel like you may need extra support to explore this more, look for a professional therapist to help you along the way.

Part 1

1
Happiness - Have you found it yet?

Something most of us are searching for is happiness; we either want to become it or reach it. For as long as I can remember, I was a serial happiness chaser, regularly changing things up as I headed to Utopia! I thought happiness was the purpose of life! We are constantly bombarded with messages and hundreds of self-help tools all urging us to find happiness or show us how we can achieve it. I found striving to be happy and looking to find happiness was exhausting and left me feeling unfulfilled. The fabulous Russ Harris, author of The Happiness Trap, helped me to rethink how I viewed happiness. Happiness can be looked at in two ways, as a good feeling that we chase or as Carl Rogers said – A way of being.

Spending your life chasing endless experiences of happiness will make you feel unsatisfied.

I don't know about you but I'm not happy all–the time and that's ok, I now find it so helpful to see happiness as a way of being and something that's not fixed. It's helpful because when I'm happy I savour the moment and when I am sad or anxious, I know it will pass. You can't be happy - or any emotion all the time - as life comes with a variety of emotions and whilst you want to mainly feel good, the truth is that your life will involve all the other emotions at any given time. You will, at some point, encounter loss, separation, rejection, illness, or infirmity. Being aware and going through the emotions instead of chasing happiness will help you face your challenges. Being distracted by chasing happiness may cause you more anxiety in the long run, as you could be blindsided when you have to deal with the other things that happen to you as a part of life.

You are wild, you are

We humans have strong instincts, and they help us to make decisions. They are extremely helpful when it comes to relationships and developing opinions. Considering how they influence you, can help you to understand your behaviour. Instincts are stronger than logic or intellect, so it's important that you know how and when they are taking over. Here are some common human instincts:

- Preferring Ease and Safety: Opting for comfort and avoiding danger.
- Social Connectivity: Our inherent need to belong and associate with others.
- Fear of the Unknown: Perceiving the new or unfamiliar as potentially hazardous.
- Quick Judgement for Survival: Using profiling to identify friends or foes rapidly.
- Jealously and Envy: Related to rivalry, but more personal.
- Shyness and Sociability: Introverts and extroverts happen naturally because each has a role to play in the hierarchy.
- Productivity: Creating, building, and making things keeps a community strong.
- Desire to be Great or Important: The need to 'matter' runs deep.

Understanding how your instinct affects you in everyday life will help you make sense of the seemingly uncontrollable and powerful feelings you will often get. Being self-led in these moments means you can notice a big emotion and that your instinct is involved in how you are responding to a situation. The flood of signals has activated your 'fear response' so what do you do? Can you take this feeling as a signal from your body as a sign to relax? Try to think of a visual that can help you; perhaps the ocean, trees, or a calm person, I think of my husband, he's usually calm and collected.

Let go, this is easier said than done, because you may be experiencing things in your body, like your heart racing and so on. Your mind will have flooded you with thoughts to warn you about the situation, so you need to create some space and break the cycle.

- Focus on your body: What is happening? What is tight? Are you shaking?
- Do some box breathing, inhale, counting 1, 2, 3, and 4, and then exhale, counting 1, 2, 3, 4, 5, and 6, then inhale again, counting 1, 2, 3, and 4, and then exhale again, counting 1, 2, 3, 4, 5, and 6; this establishes a rhythm.

At the same time, invite the breath to be even or smooth, meaning that the volume of the breath stays consistent as it moves in and out, like sipping liquid through a narrow straw. If you manage this for just a few minutes, the breath helps you remain present.

Paying attention to your body regenerates balance faster, restoring your ability to think, listen, and relate. This takes practice, but eventually, you can retrain yourself to respond rather than to react. Anger or frustration can become clarity, sadness can lead to compassion and these big emotions can become a fuel for change.

Connection

Connection can be amazing; when we feel connected with others, we feel safe, it promotes well-being and helps us stay motivated. But the strong instinct to connect can also have a massive impact on your life, from your use of social media to the power structure we live in. While connection brings huge benefits, it also can cause challenges in today's society. You are hard-wired to want to connect, which means that this instinct may often overrule your logic, for example, the desire to fit in and be accepted by a group. Or staying in a toxic relationship due to the fear of loneliness or abandonment.

Being self-led means you will consider your strong instincts and make sure you are making connections aligned with your personal values. Scan your behaviour and make sure you are not overruling your logic.

I reflect on how the desperate need for connection influenced my life in many ways. It made sense when I learned how my need for belonging would often overrule my head and heart. We all need to connect, and I think it's sometimes used by people as a way of getting you to behave or follow the rules.

If you don't do what someone says, they might threaten to leave you, ignore you or remove you from a group. My earliest memory of fearing the loss of connection was when I was sent to my room by my parents or told to go away, 'children should be seen and not heard'. I wanted to be loved and accepted by my parents, so I toed the line and followed their rules.

School - the sh!t show

I was bullied for the first few years of High School; two boys would make fun of how thin my legs were and call me 'Ricketts'. I also have an olive skin complexion, and they would constantly call me racist names. This bullying went on for years until finally, I retaliated. I still remember the emotional pain I felt for being made fun of and not being accepted during those school years, it was awful. Can you see how past experiences of being bullied at school or work, can continue to affect how you connect with yourself and others in the future? There were many questionable choices I made throughout my teenage years, all of which stemmed from my need to connect and be accepted. With self-awareness you can spot your own patterns and be able to identify any old feelings and any outdated beliefs that you need to update.

Hindsight

I wish I had known the most important connection of all was with myself. I can't change the past. However, I can become more aware of my choices today and how my past experiences can influence me. I know that I still deeply crave connection, which, ironically, I don't find easy as I also struggle with trusting people. Being self-led helps me to make sure that I am connecting in meaningful relationships that make me feel safe and support my well-being, and they bring all of the qualities that will help me to flourish.

Are you congru-what?

In person-centred therapy, we often use the word congruence, which means being real, authentic, and genuine. It is called congruence because your inner experience and outward expression match. When the therapist is authentic, they are more trustworthy, which helps to build a good therapeutic relationship with clients.

The opposite is incongruence, this is when there is a misalignment and not a balance or overlap between your real self and the ideal self. Basically, when your inside and outside don't match, i.e., you're not living the life you want or suppressing parts of yourself, you may become anxious or question who you are. If this is the case its likely you will struggle with self-image and self-esteem.

Research suggests that being authentic can be key to a person's well-being, authenticity has also been shown to provide a buffering effect against stress and distress when facing a challenge or conflict.

Reaching your full potential

Think of the seed. You know that there is a point at which you will start to grow into a flower, but now the question is how do you reach this point?

I find these two ideas helpful to discuss with clients as they get you thinking about, 'Are you following a process'? 'Do you feel you have a power that pushes you'?

Some psychologists describe self-actualisation as 'becoming everything you can become' or 'the best version of yourself'. Some psychologists believe you have a longing that is automatically built into you from birth that instinctively pushes you to grow. Being a human is having that natural urge to strive and push forward guided by an invisible force unique to us. How we grow is unique to each person, often this power may be hidden behind our thinking and negative beliefs.

On the other hand, Abraham Maslow believed that to get to the point where you have reached your full potential, you must first go through the five stages in the diagram.

Maslow's Hierarchy of Needs

In Maslow's hierarchy of needs, self-actualisation (reaching your full potential) is placed at the very top of the triangle. He believes reaching the point of self-actualisation can be achieved by first attending to your basic needs like food, water, and shelter. You can then move on to sorting your employment, health, and property and then move on to building friendships and connections. The process will lead you to self-esteem, but as this is the final stage, and as there are 5 stages, not all people will get there.

WHHHHAAAATT....? Not ALL of us will make it?

Carl Rogers on the other hand believed in something slightly different. He called it the actualising tendency, the motivating *force* behind your behaviour.

He believed reaching your potential is not an end goal

reserved for a select few, as Maslow's theory suggested. Rogers believes you are born with it and your life begins with a longing (motivation) to reach completeness in your way. He says your growth is affected by your environment and the people you are surrounded by. Here is the seed again, I often talk to my clients about Rogers' famous story about a potato, it's a great way to explain Actualising Tendency and helped me to get it!

Have you ever left a potato in a dark cupboard, not realised, and then one day you opened the cupboard and noticed huge sprouts? I think they can look quite creepy, but it's rather fascinating. Those long, ugly sprouts start as little white nubs (eyes) that then grow into huge, thwarted stems, they grow in the dark, taking advantage of any small cracks of light available in the cupboard. Whenever the door is opened and some light enters, it encourages the eyes to grow, they fight for survival. The eye of the potato was growing into a stem because that's what it does. Despite the environment, it was striving for the light and if you were to plant that potato in some soil where it should be, you would soon find green sprouts pushing through the surface, followed by flourishing green leaves. So, the environment dictated how the potato grew, but in both examples, it was growing. Rogers says we can see the same desire to lean toward growth/light in ourselves. Even in a dark environment, there's still an urge to grow.

Which theory do you lean into?

Do you think you need to achieve certain things before you are self-actualised, or do you think you have been born with the desire to push despite the circumstances?

Or both?

I sit somewhere in the middle, leaning towards Rogers, but find some comfort in both theories. I relate with the idea that you may need the correct foundations to achieve certain things. However, it can lead to thinking you must follow a set of processes and if you fail at one stage, you won't reach the end goal. My friend and I often joke about achieving level one; especially after having children when I wasn't meeting my basic needs, showers and food went out of the window and no surprise I felt rubbish.

I found comfort and believe that we all naturally want to become the best version of who we are. Through research I found inside my very essence, deep inside my own body, there is a force that's willing me to push forward.

Summary

- We all experience being cracked open differently and it's common to carry on while you work on fixing yourself.
- The needs that were met or not in your early years can give clues to any feelings that show later in life.
- Incongruence is when your outside doesn't match your inside.
- Some Psychologists believe you are born with an instinct to grow towards your goals.
- Two different theories around being self-actualised (Maslow) and the actualising tendency (Rogers)
- A question to ponder, do you need to hit certain milestones before you reach your full potential?

2
Self-care - Make it a personal requirement

It is a phrase we can't escape from and something I now take very seriously; The British Association for Counselling and Psychotherapy guidelines suggest practising self-care as part of the ethical framework for therapists, and I can see why. Not only does practising self-care set a great example to others, but it also fills your thinking with messages like 'you are worthy' and 'doing things you love makes you happy'.

Being 'cracked open' and vulnerable can feel raw and lonely. It's important that you start as you mean to go on, part of living a Self-Led Life® involves considering yourself and making the time to practise self-care. I am not just talking about hot bubble baths and spas; I mean taking the time to purposefully think about your unique version of self-care and creating a personal plan will help you strengthen your foundations. Having a plan will help you manage anxiety and help navigate burn-in! Self-care is personal to you, so it's important that you design your way of creating a space that will support your growth and help to enhance your awareness. Once you have uncovered what self-care means to you, you will be able to create your own intentional and sustainable routine.

Insights:

Later, you will examine other areas of your self-care, such as setting boundaries, etc, in more detail. However, for now, let's focus on some quick tools you can use and some tips to handle any anxious or tense moments, remember to use the book companion as there's a section for you to keep all of this handy.

What are my go-to things?

Take a break to enjoy a cup of tea, take some deep breaths, journal, go for a short walk, call or send a voice note to a friend, or look at something that brings you happiness.

I cannot stress enough the power of writing, even if it's just for five minutes a day. Somehow, the magic happens as the paper gives voice to your true self. The words you write are clues, hints, tips, and motivation all waiting to be heard. We all have an inner voice, your owl, waiting to be heard - all you need to do is give it some space and listen.

Another great exercise in being self-led is to look at what your basic foundations are, these are the things that you need to do to feel good. What are yours, as well as food, and shelter, what else do you need to include in your life to help you feel good? This could be a walk, a run, reading, connecting with someone, or listening to music. The aim is for you to create a set of foundations that include all things you know will help you to feel good. Like Maslow-but think of yours like a foundation of bricks, each one contains a basic need that you have. Being aware of what helps will provide extra awareness on your journey of growth and be mindful of what makes you feel good. If you're feeling a little off, this awareness will help you to refocus and get back on track, making time for your basics. Your foundations are also a great conversation topic to have with your partner or loved ones. While you share what's important to you it can lead to further conversations around what support you may need. It is also a great way to give support to someone else, ask your partner or a friend what their basic needs are, and check in regularly. If you or a friend or partner are not managing to practise self-care, then perhaps you help one another? If you haven't made time for that run, bath, or thing that you need can you step in and help one another to give the space and time you need? Make sure that basic needs are revisited, as they may change, be self-led and check in with yourself regularly. You can also explore why you're not getting what you need by journaling; be honest with yourself, look at what's getting in your way and if necessary, reach out for help.

Self-aware as self-care

"Knowing yourself is the beginning of wisdom."

— *Aristotle*

Consider for a moment the idea of leading your own life. It is something that often gets overshadowed by the daily grind and the weight of external expectations. Living a Self-Led Life® isn't just about making choices; it's about ensuring those choices authentically reflect who you are, beyond the pressures of everyday life.

You might wonder, 'How do I get there?' The key lies in self-awareness. This isn't just about reflection; it's about recognising self-awareness as a radical act of self-care. More than indulging in relaxation or treats, self-awareness involves a deeper engagement with your emotions, beliefs, and values.

In a world overflowing with opinions on how you should live, self-awareness becomes your stable guide. It helps you to understand and align with your emotions, beliefs, and values. This alignment isn't just helpful for making authentic life choices; it's also a form of self-care. After all, truly understanding and accepting yourself is perhaps the greatest kindness you can offer yourself.

How does self-awareness play a role in personal growth?

The answer lies in its power to inform and guide your life choices. When you're self-aware, you have a clearer understanding of what truly makes you happy, what drains your energy, and what motivates you. This knowledge is invaluable because it steers you towards choices that resonate with your authentic self. It is like having an internal compass that helps you navigate through life's complexities and challenges.

But there's another part, it’s a profound form of self-care. Often, we think of self-care in terms of physical well-being, like exercise and nutrition. However, taking care of your mental and emotional health is just as important. Self-awareness creates this care by encouraging you to acknowledge and accept your feelings and thoughts. It allows you to celebrate your strengths and gently work on your weaknesses without judgement. Embracing self-awareness can lead to healthier and more authentic life choices. It is about being honest with yourself and making decisions that align with your true values and aspirations. This authenticity not only brings clarity and fulfilment but also nurtures your mental and emotional well-being.

"Who looks outside, dreams; who looks inside, awakes."

— Carl Jung

Emotional Intelligence

At the core of self-awareness lies emotional intelligence. This is your ability to understand and manage your emotions. By becoming emotionally intelligent, you're not just reacting to feelings as they come. Instead, you're recognising, processing, and responding to them in a way that's both healthy and constructive. This is a crucial form of emotional self-care. When you're attuned to your emotions, you can better handle stress, communicate effectively, and empathise with others, enriching both your personal and professional life.

Values and Beliefs

Your values and beliefs shape who you are. Aligning your actions with these core principles is a vital aspect of living authentically. When your life reflects what you truly believe in, you experience a sense of harmony and satisfaction. This alignment is a form of self-care because it respects and nurtures your deepest sense of self. It is about making choices that resonate with your innermost beliefs, rather than conforming to external expectations or societal norms.

Self-Awareness as the Foundation of a Self-Led Life®

Self-awareness is more than just a part of a self-led life; it's the very foundation. When you deeply understand your thoughts, feelings, and behaviours, you're better equipped to make choices that genuinely reflect your values and aspirations. This understanding leads to deliberate and fulfilling life choices, steering you towards a life that feels authentically yours.

Self-Awareness For Life

Embracing self-awareness is not a one-time event but a continuous journey. Life is dynamic, and as you grow and change, so do your needs and desires. Continuous self-reflection and adaptation are vital practices in this lifelong commitment to self-care. It's about regularly checking in with yourself, being open to change, and making adjustments as needed.

Staying true to yourself during life's ever-changing circumstances is an ongoing act of self-care. It requires patience, resilience, and the willingness to sometimes stand against the 'norm'. The key is to remember that as your life evolves, your understanding of yourself should also evolve.

The importance of self-awareness in living a self-led and self-cared life cannot be overstated. It is the cornerstone of personal authenticity and well-being. Remember that each step of self-awareness is a step towards a more fulfilled and contented life. Embrace this journey with an open heart and mind, knowing that it is one of the most rewarding journeys you will ever undertake. Your path to a Self-Led Life® is unique and entirely your own, and every step you take in understanding and caring for yourself is a step towards a life that is richly and beautifully yours.

3
Self-concept and Well-being

"We see the world not as it is, but as we are."

— Covey (2004: 28)

Your Self-Concept is how you see yourself and the perception you have about your abilities.

Who are you? What makes you, you?

You may respond, I'm a mother, or I am a student, maybe I am a successful painter, or even I am kind and generous or I am hard-working.

These responses come from your internal sense of who you are. This sense is developed from childhood and goes through constant evaluation and adjustment throughout your entire life.

You form and manage your self-concept as you grow based on the knowledge you have about yourself. It is multidimensional, for example, you may have a very different idea of who you are in terms of your physical body, and who you are in terms of your spirit or soul.

The self-concept is an important guiding principle that helps you navigate the world and understand your role in it. Parts of your self-concept may be good or not-so-good for your well-being. That is why learning more about your self-concept is an essential part of living a Self-Led Life®

This book is an extension of my research into authenticity and is based on the principles of Carl Rogers who believed our self-concept is made up of three parts which are the foundations of the book. He suggests that all three parts must work together to achieve congruence which helps you to be authentic. However, when all these parts are not in harmony or disconnected, it can lead to feelings of anxiety or tension, which is referred to as incongruence.

1. Self-Image - Who you are today
2. Ideal Self - Who you aspire to be
3. Self-Worth - How you feel about yourself

Self-Concept and Congruence Vs Incongruence

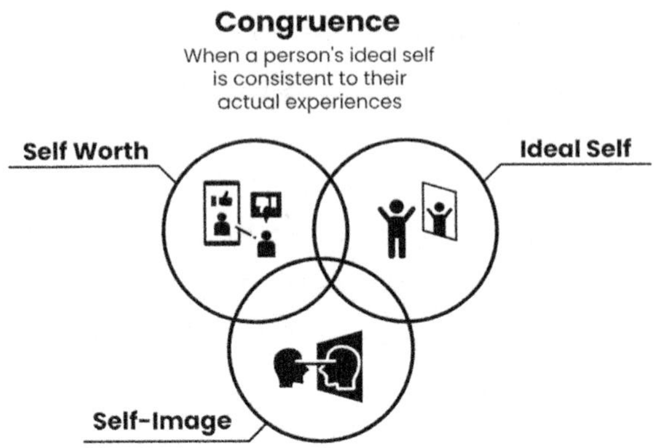

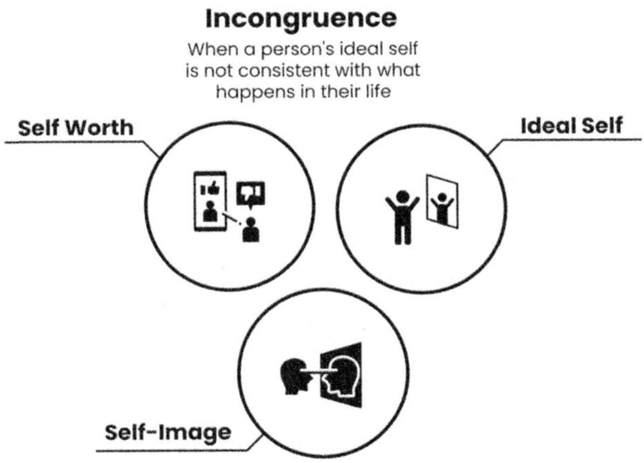

The aim of exploring all three parts is to move towards being more congruent and authentic and in doing so you are better equipped to live a 'good life' as more of an ongoing state as opposed to a destination.

Research suggests that successful or self-directed people often exhibit a state of congruence. There are lots of theories around exactly what the self-concept is; broadly, it's accepted that.

- Self-concept is the overall idea we have about who we are and includes cognitive and affective judgements about ourselves.
- It is learned, not inherent.
- Self-concept develops through childhood and early adulthood when it is more easily changed or updated.

(Source: PositivePsychology.com)

Let's take a closer look at the three parts.

Self-image is a powerful perception that shapes your view of yourself. It reflects your experiences, the feedback you receive, and your perception of how others view you. It encompasses physical attributes, social roles, personality traits, and more. When there is a difference between your self-image and your true self, it can create anxiety and tension. However, with the right mindset and support, you can overcome this challenge and develop a healthy and confident self-image.

Ideal Self: This is the person you aspire to be. It is a constructed image based on your life experiences, societal expectations, and personal aspirations. The Ideal Self includes the traits and achievements that you wish to have. According to Rogers, a significant gap between the Ideal Self and the Real Self can lead to dissatisfaction and psychological tension.

Self-worth: Your self-worth, or self-esteem, is about how much you value yourself and your sense of being worthy. Rogers stressed that having strong self-worth means you're better equipped to handle life's challenges and less swayed by what others think. You view yourself as deserving of happiness and are confident in your ability to reach your goals. When your self-image aligns well with your ideal self, your self-worth usually increases, boosting your overall happiness and emotional health.

Looking at yourself in three parts can help you understand how they all need to be nourished equally. You may notice that you have experienced feeling tense if there seems to be a gap between the person you are and who you aspire to be. This also highlights the need to pay attention to your self-esteem, the trick here is to try and make sure you have balance in each of these areas. It is great to have an idea of the person you aspire to be but if you struggle to look in the mirror the chances are it's going to be a struggle.

Summary

- Congruence is when all three parts overlap.
- Tension or anxiety can be felt when these parts are not in harmony with one another.
- Any gaps can be used to highlight further learning.

Self-Led Life® Inspired actions

- Regular check-in and clock which parts need your extra focus.
- Look at ways to develop in each of these areas.
- Confront self-esteem and get extra support if required.
- Look at ways to get in touch with your ideal self to better know the future you.

Exploring Yourself and Your Congruence

This insight will help get a deeper understanding of your three parts and identify any gaps between them. Answer the following questions to gain insights into how closely your self-image aligns with your ideal self and how both reflect your true self. The greater the alignment, the more congruent and authentic your life experience.

Use your handy book companion to help you complete the information.

Understanding Your Three Selves: Self Image, Ideal Self, and Self Worth

Self Image:

- Perception Analysis: Write down your views about yourself and how you think friends, family, and colleagues perceive you.
- Reality Check: Compare these views with who you really are and identify the differences.

Ideal Self:

- Description: Define your 'Ideal Self.' What are your aspirations, core values, and the key traits you wish to embody? Describe the life you aim to lead.
- Visualisation: Picture a perfect day in your ideal life. What are you doing? How do you feel? Who are you with?

Self Worth:

- Self-Assessment: Reflect on your current status. What are your strengths and areas for improvement? What have you accomplished so far?

- Honest Reflection: Evaluate yourself honestly, acknowledging the good and the areas needing work without judgement.

PART 2: BRIDGING THE GAPS

- Compare your ideal self with your self-image (real self). Are there any differences?
- Focus on specific areas where your self-image differs from your ideal self.

Understanding Discrepancies:

- Reflect on the reasons behind these gaps. Consider internal conflicts, fears, or external pressures.

Explore Congruence:

This insight aims to help you understand congruence — the alignment between your inner feelings and thoughts, and your outward expressions and behaviours.

- Think of a recent situation where you experienced a strong emotion. It could be happiness, anger, sadness, excitement, etc.
- Write down the emotion you felt during that situation.
- Now, reflect on how you expressed this emotion

outwardly. Did you express it directly (e.g., through words, facial expressions, body language), suppress it, or express something different?

- Compare your inner emotion with your outward expression. Ask yourself were they aligned (congruent)?
- If not, why might you have expressed it differently?
- How did it feel to express or not express this emotion?

Reflection:

Spend a few minutes reflecting on your findings. Consider what influenced your level of congruence in that situation. Were there external factors (like social norms, the presence of certain people), or internal factors (like fear of judgement, trying to protect someone's feelings)?

****Please remember these tools are just that, they are to help guide you and should not be treated as medical advice ****

4
What glasses are you wearing?

"We see the world not as it is but as we are."

— Anais Nin

As you have learned, your self-concept is your internal view of yourself and your beliefs about your abilities and worth. Your frame of reference, meanwhile, is the mental framework that shapes how you interpret your experiences, influenced by your history, culture, and values. Understanding how they fit together helps in personal growth and developing empathy, recognising that everyone's view of the world is unique to your self-concept and frame of reference.

Think of your self-concept as your profile, like the one you have on social media. It's the collection of details about you—what you're good at, what you look like, what you believe, and what's important to you. It is like your personal brand.

Your frame of reference is like the filter you use on your camera or the settings in your favourite video game. It changes the way you see things around you. So, when things happen, the frame of reference is how you interpret it—kind of like choosing whether to see it in a positive light, a negative one, or somewhere in between.

We all have unique experiences

Any police officer will tell you two people who saw the same event will describe it in very different ways. We all see the world differently, and each person holds different values and beliefs and looks at the world through those individual values and beliefs. Throughout your life, you have walked your own path and, as a result, have gained a unique set of experiences.

You have subconsciously been busy gathering and storing information since you were born through many sources, such as:

- Messages from society.
- Relationships you have with parents/family/primary caregivers.
- The culture you are born into.
- The beliefs that are instilled in you.

- How you are expected to act or interact based on your gender.

Over time, this huge amount of data has all come together and created your truths about who you believe you are and life in general. It is so important to have an understanding of what information and messages you have collected, as this is the very source of knowledge that you draw upon every day. Each time you decide what to do, what to buy and also how you interact with people it's all drawn from here, it's the information you use to form an opinion.

You can also think of your frame of reference as a pair of glasses, the frame being a set of beliefs that are only personal to you, and the lens you look through is how you see the world. You are not always aware of the information that your frame is made from and how it influences what you see through your lenses; it's the thinking behind the thinking, a part that naturally ticks over.

Frame of reference

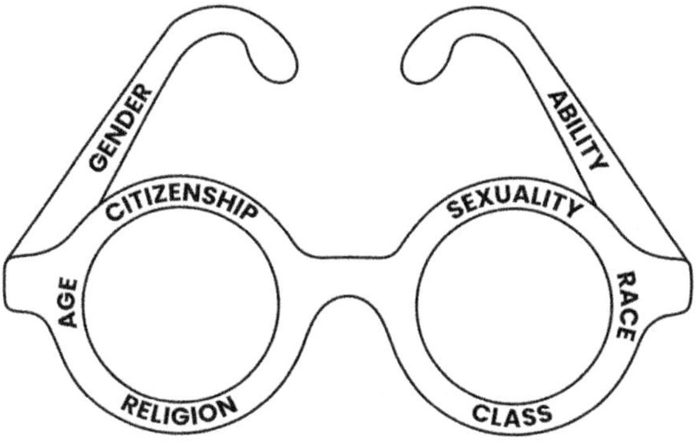

To know and be able to lead yourself effectively, you need to know about how your frame of reference influences your thinking and the impact it's having on your everyday life, relationships, and decision-making. This often-hidden knowledge can help you better understand others and make positive changes in your relationships.

Therapists learn to be aware and mindful of their frame of reference, I found this awareness has followed me outside of the therapy room too. I think we can all learn the importance of being aware of our perspectives, and the ability to be flexible with understanding other people's needs. Learning just how different we all are was a real learning curve; I'll be honest that I sometimes really question giving or receiving advice, we really do have to take it with a pinch of salt. I am not saying it doesn't come in handy to ask for people's opinions, but new awareness teaches us that the advice we get will be unique to that person's view and if you're dependent on the advice of others you're not growing and learning to lean into your sense of perspective. The best thing to do is make sure before acting on advice is to check that it aligns with YOUR values. If you have low self-worth and need validation from people before making a decision it will be like spinning a roulette wheel - depending on who you ask will determine the outcome.

Knowing when someone is stuck in their frame and knowing when yours is getting in the way is a game changer. Being aware of frames of reference is crucial for effective communication, conflict resolution, decision-making, personal growth, cultural sensitivity, collaboration, and reducing biases. It helps in navigating a world where people come from diverse backgrounds and have different experiences and perspectives.

Summary

- Your frame of reference is made up of your thoughts/beliefs and forms the lenses through which you and only **you** view the world.
- It is also referred to as your reality filter, which can be activated anytime.
- Everyone's frame is unique depending upon their different experiences.

Self-Led Life® inspired actions

- Developing your own belief in leading yourself
- Being aware of others' frame when communicating and checking that the advice is aligned with your values.
- Understanding how unique we all are and appreciating other people's views.

This insight exercise will help to start the process of identifying and understanding your frame of reference and the practice of considering those of others. It will help you to lay out a foundation of your understanding of your personal beliefs and where they have originated from. Grab your book companion and find somewhere comfy. This is insightful and powerful; remember that the work you put in will be worth it as you find out who you THINK you are.

Place:

- How has the country/region in which you lived influenced how you see the world?
- What languages do you speak?
- Have you always lived in the same country, and if so, how does that shape what you see?
- How diverse was the area you grew up in?
- What message(s) about where you grew up gives you about your values?

Class:

- How did your class background (poor, working class, middle class etc.) shape your expectations of the future? What do you believe you can achieve?
- What resources do you have access to?
- How do you talk, dress etc.?

Religion:

- Were you raised with a certain tradition?
- How did it shape you?
- What kind of framework did (does) it provide you?
- What is the relationship between your religion and the dominant culture you are in?

Race:

- Did you grow up with a sense of yourself as a member of a racial group?
- Did other people respond to you in that way?
- How did it shape your place in the world?

Body:

- How do aspects of your body influence your orientation to the world?
- How do others treat you?
- How do definitions of 'what's normal' shape your identity with your body?
- How about skin colour too?

Gender:

- What messages from society did you get about what it meant to be your assigned gender?
- What roles and expectations did others have of you based on gender?
- What appears to be 'open' to you based on gender?
- How does your gender shape your daily experience and routine?

Sexuality:

- How does your sexuality shape how you see the world? How do you define yourself?
- Your expectations in life, your partners, your family?
- How do others see you?
- What rights and privileges do you, or don't you, have access to?

Family:

- How did your family shape you?
- Consider birth order.
- Family changes over time?

Have you identified some key experiences that you can identify that have shaped how you view the world? Add your notes and any lightbulb moments to your book companion.

5
The NEED to defend

Hopefully, you are now aware that you have acquired a set of beliefs shaped by your self-concept, taking into account your unique frame of reference that has all formed your thinking. Phew! Things are about to get even more interesting. What do you think happens if something or someone challenges those embedded beliefs?

A spiky ordeal

I will tell you what ... It can be a spiky ordeal! When your self-concept is challenged, you will instinctively jump to defend it, and quite often, you will cling on for dear life like you're on a white-knuckle ride. Why? Because as we have learned your self-concept is shaped by your beliefs, it's fundamentally who you are. Remember our instinct, this is where we get to see it in action, the need to survive kicks in here. If your self-concept is questioned, it feels unsteady, unfamiliar, and unsafe. Your brain likes to keep you safe, it doesn't like to be wrong as imperfections feel like danger, and so it will go in to defense mode. So, you're naturally wired to keep your self-concept safe, but it can also mean you won't accept some information you hear as true as it's not 'true to you'. This can cause disagreements as you have a reaction to information that is not in line with your beliefs. Your brain will eagerly search for ways to confirm the information that you have stored IS the truth, as your self-concept must stay safe!

Beliefs

One of the beliefs that you might have identified is the idea that hard work equals money. This belief could have been ingrained in you through watching your parents or caregivers work hard, as well as being exposed to messages from society which reinforce this message. As a result, you may have developed a view that you must work hard to earn money, which has now become a belief. You wouldn't necessarily go about your daily life talking about this view; it's just there until it's activated, then it can cause you to feel spiky and trigger the need to defend, this whole process is often unconscious until it kicks in.

Imagine you are having a conversation with a friend, and the friend mentions they have started a new and exciting business venture which has made a huge profit in the first few months. They are surprised they haven't had to work hard, in fact, they said it was easy. As this situation doesn't match a belief that you have embedded, it can trigger a response, you may feel a little discomfort as you feel the need to defend your belief, making sure your self-concept is safe and doesn't panic because of the contradictory information you are hearing. It cannot be possible to earn money that easily! You may experience a strong feeling that it is necessary that you are right and your mission, remember, is to always keep that self-concept intact. Hearing that your friend has had easy success has caused you to feel uncomfortable; as a result, you will consciously or subconsciously defend or challenge your own beliefs.

The mission has begun

Here is an example of a few different reactions you may have:

The spike - A real pointy reaction to something that challenges your self-concept can be seen in arguments when people hang onto their opposite views for dear life. You may respond with a disagreement, telling your friend that it sounds too good to be true, accuse them of lying, or play it down with a 'just you wait' response.

The self-check and challenge - You may be able to conduct a quick self-audit and challenge yourself and that embedded belief without even noticing and feel authentic pride with a good-for-her attitude.

The avoider - which is common, you tend to avoid conflict, so you may not say anything at the time and choose to tell someone else the story, you return home to your partner or call a friend and tell them all about your friend's experience and how and why it cannot be true (based on your beliefs). It simply cannot be that easy; your truth is correct. They will need to work hard, and at some point, hard work will catch up with your friend. In this example, you have self-soothed that spiky feeling from the moment; you feel better and relaxed now that you have justified why your belief is correct. Your self-concept is safely intact without arguing, it's a win-win for it!

Daily protection

Defending your self-concept is an everyday occurrence for your brain, that is why it's important to remember that those beliefs, things that are true to you, are only true for you. They have been formed subconsciously depending upon the unique journey you have walked.

They may well need updating, but how will you know unless you are aware of them? Until they are explored, they will remain true and a part of you. Feeling spikey and the need to defend your beliefs gives you a little internal nudge to do a self-audit to check if the belief is worth staying or needs updating?

Having an understanding that everyone generally acts on the need to be right and will defend their own beliefs can help you understand why people tend to act defensively. Hopefully, this will help you meet a spikey person with more compassion. Knowing how you typically react when you are triggered will also allow you to make a conscious choice of how to respond in these moments.

Summary

- We naturally defend something that threatens our 'belief system'
- If a belief is questioned, you may respond in three ways: spike, challenge, or avoid.
- Your brain is constantly working to protect your self-concept.

Self-Led Life® Inspired actions

- Pay attention to your spikey moments and see them as an opportunity to grow, look out and get curious.
- Being aware that any spikey reaction gives you the opportunity to practise compassion.
- When you notice a spike conduct a quick self-audit and challenge your embedded thinking.

This insight will help you find out what triggers you to defend and how you react or not, helping you to increase your awareness of yourself and others.

- When was the last time you felt unjust or the need to defend?
- Did you defend yourself in that moment or remove yourself and justify your view?
- How did you respond?
- How did you feel after?

Keep a log of the last few spikes or triggers that you have had, can you spot any themes, is it when someone mentions work, family, lifestyle etc? This is all leaning into a little more awareness, so having an idea of what is likely to cause a spike will help you manage how you react.

**This insight is regarding spikey reactions to everyday beliefs, I have not specifically mentioned trauma responses in this book, please seek advice or support if you need any trauma specific support **

6
Focus on the Locus

You may imagine a swarm of locusts, but there are no insects here. However, there is another type of pest that may be getting in your way; your locus of control. This means the extent to which you believe you have control over your behaviour and influence your thoughts, feelings, and actions. By having an awareness of your locus and adjusting it, you can unlock a more empowered approach to any challenges.

You have two types of locus which underpin your thoughts and beliefs, your **internal** locus and your **external** locus.

- If you use your internal locus, it means you have greater personal control, and you are generally proactive in getting things done.
- If you use your external locus, it means you tend

to blame others and are more passive and accepting.

Internal - Active	External - Passive
I can decide my own future.	There isn't much I can do about my future.
My passion and hard work help me to achieve my goals.	Why bother, whatever is meant to be will be.
I am in control of my life.	I accept, I go with the flow, and other factors such as luck, and fate control me.

Knowing which locus to focus on-can affect not only how you react to the events in your life, but also your drive to take inspired action. If you believe that you have the power to determine your fate, you are much more likely to make changes in your life when needed-such as; making decisions confidently about your business, career or lifestyle. Equally, if you think that the outcome of events are determined by chance, you will be less motivated to take action towards making positive changes. It is important to focus on your internal locus of control, especially during times of self-doubt. According to research, there is a consensus that people with a higher level of internal locus of control tend to have better outcomes. It is essential to keep in mind that it's not set in stone, having an internal locus of control doesn't always guarantee positive outcomes. Similarly, having an external locus of control doesn't necessarily lead to negative results. The good news is psychologists believe that locus of control is learned and it's not a case of being internal or external but rather drifting between the two so ongoing focus on the locus will help!

How will it help you?

If you believe that your actions have a direct effect on the outcomes in your life, you're likely to see some real benefits such as:

Career: You'll take charge of your job path, seeking promotions and opportunities to grow because you know your efforts make a difference.

Health: You'll likely eat better, exercise, feeling responsible for your well-being.

Learning: In school or any learning environment, you'll put in the work and ask for help when needed, understanding that this will help you succeed.

Stress: When things get tough, you'll tackle problems head-on, managing stress better because you believe you can control the situation.

Relationships: You'll work on your relationships, knowing that what you do can improve or fix issues with friends, family, or partners.

Finances: You'll budget and save, confident that your financial health is in your hands.

Personal Goals: Setting goals and working on self-improvement come naturally to you, as you see personal growth as something you control.

Mental Health: You're more likely to stay mentally healthy–or seek support when you need it since you understand your role in managing your mental state.

Environment: You'll do your part for the planet, recycling and saving energy, because you feel your actions are part of a bigger change.

Do you have an external or internal locus of control?

Where does your locus of control fall? Read through the statements below and select the set that best describes your outlook on life.

External locus of control - If you agree with the statements, you likely have an external locus of control.

- I often feel like I have little control over my life and the things that happen to me.
- It's common for people to not receive what they truly deserve.

- It is not worth setting goals or making plans because too many things can happen that are outside of my control.
- Life is a game of chance; it is unpredictable and is subject to random events that are beyond my control.
- I have little influence over the events of the world.

Internal locus of control - If you agree with the below, you likely have an internal locus of control.

- My efforts determine my success.
- I am responsible for the choices I make and their consequences.
- My actions can create positive change in my life.
- Challenges are opportunities for growth.
- I am capable of finding solutions to the problems I face.

These answers are a clue about how you experience your day-to-day life. If your results point towards an internal locus of control, it's self-leadership and shows your belief in your power to shape your future. If they reveal an external locus of control, consider this a nudge to get aware, reclaim your control, and gently shift the balance of power from the world around you to the world within you.

Think of your locus of control as the GPS for your life's road trip. If you've got an internal locus, you're in the driver's seat, picking your routes and destinations. It's like knowing you're the one who decides whether to take the scenic route or the fast lane, influencing your journey as you go.

The internal locus of control in action

Embracing an internal locus of control infuses your daily routine with empowerment. Imagine: you're hit with an unexpected bill or an issue at work just as your day starts. Instead of sinking into frustration, you tap into your inner compass. You are strategising before the tea is done brewing—reshuffling budgets, tweaking timelines, reaching out. This influence is quiet yet purposeful. In heated meetings or heart-to-hearts with a friend in need, this inner guidance system gives you the clarity to look for solutions, you're calm and transformative, steering situations, not just coasting along.

The external locus of control in action

Those days when it feels like you're just along for the ride. That is an external locus of control for you. When you get hit with the unexpected bill it's not just an annoyance—it feels like the universe is out to get you. In meetings, instead of jumping in, you might find yourself sitting on the sidelines, waiting to see how conversations play out. Your downtime is also a mirror of this mindset. It can affect your decision to try a new skill and will limit the opportunities you give to yourself that help you get closer to your ideal self.

Helping others

Understanding the concept of locus of control in everyday life is incredibly valuable because it shapes how you interpret and respond to events around you. Being able to shift not only boosts your resilience and well-being but also allows you to support friends and family in adopting a more proactive approach to life's challenges.

How to help:

Encourage them to be self-led: Prompt them to identify actions they can take, no matter how small, to address their situation.

Affirm their strengths: Point out their successes and how their actions led to positive outcomes.

Promote problem-solving: When they face a problem, instead of giving advice, ask guiding questions that help them think of solutions themselves.

Model behaviour: Demonstrate an internal locus of control in your own life. When you talk about challenges, speak in terms of the actions you plan to take.

Provide resources: Share books, articles, or clips on personal development that discuss the power of mindset and personal agency.

Set and respect boundaries: Teach by example the importance of setting healthy boundaries, which empowers both you and them.

Practise active listening: Sometimes, just being heard can help people feel more empowered and less alone in their struggles.

While you can offer support and encouragement, each person is ultimately responsible for their growth and change. Encouragement should be offered gently, without pushing your agenda or expectations onto others.

Summary

- You have two locus of control, external and internal
- External means we are more reliant on the opinions of others.
- Internal means we trust our judgement.
- This awareness helps us to connect to others on a deeper level.
- Research suggests people with a higher level of internal locus of control tend to have better outcomes.

Self-Led Life® inspired actions

- Being aware of yourself and other people's locus will help you to manage the urge to seek validation from others.
- Knowing you can shift your locus at any time is part-living a Self-Led Life®.
- Offer support to others giving them gentle encouragement.

Research

- The term 'Locus of control' refers to how much control a person feels they have in their behaviour. A person can either have an internal or external locus of control (Rotter, 1954).
- ** Experts in the field of psychology often disagree whether differences should be attributed based on cultural differences or whether a more worldwide measure of locus of control will be more helpful when it comes to practical application.**

This insight aims to strengthen your internal locus of control or provide strategies for those with an external locus to begin to shift their perspective. Another reminder to use the free book companion available online. You can keep all these handy insights together ready for you to look at later! Visit gericarey.com.

Decision reflection journal

To help you recognise and understand decision-making patterns in your daily life. Keep a journal for one week. Write down at least one decision you make each day, how you came to that decision, and whether you felt the outcome was within your control. Reflect on these entries to identify patterns in your decision-making process.

Circle of influence

To help you visually separate between what you can control and what you cannot, draw a large circle on a piece of paper. Inside the circle, write down things you believe you have control over. Outside the circle, list the things you feel are out of your control. Use this visual to focus your energy on the areas within your circle.

The 'what if' scenario planning

To prepare for unexpected events and build confidence in your ability to handle them think of a 'what if' scenario that concerns you. Write down a plan of how you would handle it if it were to happen. This exercise helps to reinforce the understanding that you can exert control over how you respond to unforeseen challenges.

7
Conditions of worth

Conditions of worth are conditions you believe you must meet to gain acceptance, love, or positive regard from others.

Research in psychology has supported the idea that when you feel that you must meet certain conditions to be valued by others, it can undermine your self-esteem. If you believe you must always be successful or must always please others to be worthy, you may constantly strive to meet these standards, often at the expense of your own well-being and authentic self-expression.

Examples of conditions of worth are:

- Work hard to be successful.
- Put other people first.
- Men don't cry.

- Don't get angry.
- Be quiet and do as you are told.

As a child, you quickly learn what behaviours please parents, caregivers, teachers, friendship groups, and society in general. Eventually, these become introjected values - internalised ways of behaving based on the expectations of others. These beliefs may lead to unhappiness, depression, or anxiety. Being aware of the conditions that have become unhelpful will help you to stop them from influencing your thinking today. When you live a Self-Led Life® with your way of thinking you will realise that some of the conditions that you have thought to be true don't apply to you any longer.

Rules

Rules we accept as children can echo into our adult lives.

Take Sarah's example. As a child, her parents were big on instilling the message of kindness, teaching her to always let others go first. This wasn't just good manners; it was a family value. As a result, Sarah became the type of child who always hung back, the one who nodded and stepped aside, aiming for that nod of approval from her mum.

Fast forward to adulthood, and Sarah finds it tough to shake off that voice telling her '*To be liked, you've got to be selfless.*' But here's the incongruence that voice is now clashing with Sarah's True Self's need to stand her ground, to go after what she wants. It is putting dents in her confidence, creating a tug-of-war between who she is and who she was taught to be. So, is it wrong to teach kids manners? No. But the real question is, at what point does 'being selfless' start to suppress 'being you'? I am not saying we shouldn't teach children the value of courtesy. It is about balance. It is about **not letting those childhood 'shoulds' drown out your adult 'wants'.**

This isn't about pointing fingers or playing the blame game. It's about recognising those moments when your childhood programming keeps you from hitting your stride in the here and now. It's food for thought: How much of what we learned on the playground shapes your boardroom battles, personal relationships, or self-image?

Paul is a father to his young son, Harry, who is a budding football player. In Paul's eyes, Harry has the potential to outshine his peers on the pitch, and this belief has spiralled into an obsession for Paul. He is so passionately chasing this dream that he misses the signs of Harry's distress; the tears, the anxiety, the reluctance before each game. Despite this, Paul persists, pushing Harry. This single-minded drive has ripple effects. It strains Paul's interactions with other parents, as he is competitive and defensive. Internally, Paul is grappling with deep-seated beliefs about success and worth, which now manifest in his parenting. He praises Harry when he plays with maximum effort and inadvertently shames him when he *thinks* he's being lazy.

Meanwhile, Harry is struggling. His confidence dwindles as he grapples with the pressure to be the best, valuing his dad's approval above his own desires. He is being pressured into an identity of excellence, which only raises his fears. Unknowingly, Paul's own conditioned beliefs are steering this ship – and it's taking them both into stormy waters. If Paul were to take a step back and examine the tension and frustration he felt, then he might realise they stem from outdated beliefs, – conditions no longer relevant to his or Harry's worth. By acknowledging this, Paul could find a new way forward, one that aligns with both his and Harry's true well-being.

With love

Parents often guide their children with the best of intentions, hoping to prepare them for the journey of life. However, their protective instincts can sometimes become overbearing, unintentionally limiting a child's growth. They might think they are helping by saying 'be careful' or by directing them constantly, but this can restrain the children's natural curiosity and spirit. It is important to remember to raise little self-led leaders; we need to remind ourselves that children are not to be molded, directed, or tamed, but are individuals with their unique paths. In their attempts to protect the young from life's rough edges, parents might neglect the importance of allowing them to explore and learn in a free environment. When a child who once questioned boldly and laughed freely becomes cautious and subdued, parents can reflect on what's happening, are they truly supporting their growth or subconsciously suppressing the child's natural vitality?

Seen and not heard

As I shared earlier in the book '*to be accepted children must be seen and not heard* ' was a very common message in my house. I wasn't aware of how it had impacted me until I practised self-awareness while studying to be a therapist.

Through reflection I recognised the belief that '*to be accepted children must be seen and not heard* ' had shown up years previously when I worked in a corporate job.

This hidden belief started when I was around age six and it made me want to leave childhood behind as fast as I could. I remember being self-sufficient as a young child, I would often be left to my own devices and would hear "*children must be seen and not heard*" a lot.

As I listened to the grown-ups talking, I desperately remember wanting to join in, as the youngest of four and with a ten-year age gap I was on catch-up! I could feel agitation and frustration as they urged me to talk quickly, and then get out of the way. I needed to "*be clearer, get to the point, stop waffling*". All I wanted was to join in, be heard and connect. I was a chatty little soul so no wonder I was eventually led by a strong instinct to connect, and be my true self. I came to the conclusion that the sooner I could get to adulthood the quicker I would be seen and be heard.

The floodgates

I'm sure this belief and others showed up many times over my life, but on reflection, I found that it resurfaced when I was in a very vulnerable space - when I was experiencing 'cracking open'.

I was consumed with stress and anxiety due to a series of very stressful situations in my personal life coupled with the desire to climb the career ladder. The personal stress made me feel very vulnerable and in hindsight it caused me to revert into my childlike thinking. I started to become very anxious, especially during meetings. I began to hyperfocus on every word I was saying, convinced that I could read other people's minds and that they were getting bored. I would rush what I was saying and get flustered, often not making any sense, afterwards, I would sit and replay conversations in my mind as I cringed at myself. I also started to feel very intimidated by assertive people, I found myself acting like a child around them wanting to please and being unusually submissive. This was strange behaviour for me, I was an equal in a senior role, and I was being seen and heard, but I started to feel like I wasn't worthy. I would often feel like I'd given myself the ick! Then it got worse, how could I manage other people when I couldn't manage myself?

It took me a long time to feel at peace with the decision to leave the stability of a corporate job, I didn't have the tools at the time to simultaneously handle both personal stress and ambition. This is one of the reasons I share the Self-Led Leader®. I see how common it is for business owners and leaders to be hijacked by emotions because growth makes you vulnerable and it's in that space the floodgates can open.

I used the awareness we were shown in training to be a psychotherapist to identify old conditions and reflect on how they had affected some of my later experiences. I still do this if I spot anything, not to ruminate, but I enjoy connecting the dots and learning about myself and choosing to leave them behind.

A powerful insight is that there's always an opportunity to grow from the darkest of times. It's in those times that our actions and feelings hold the clues. I learned that under stressful situations I will revert to feeling young and vulnerable and that brings up a whole load of triggers and challenges for me to deal with. Using this awareness I can start to use some of the tools I am sharing with you that help me to continue to lead myself as I continue to grow.

I hope you can see this as an opportunity not to judge yourself or others, however, I do appreciate that as you start to reflect on your childhood, you may experience some strong emotions. Are these emotions signs of conditions? Perhaps they are showing you that some beliefs are now not aligned with your ideal self. As you step towards living a more Self-Led Life®, lean into your new awareness and remember you have the power to leave them behind. Understanding the concept of conditions of worth can be an integral part of leading your own life.

Recognising your conditions of worth can help you to:

Identify limiting beliefs: By understanding the conditions you've internalised, you can identify which beliefs are holding you back. For instance, if you believe you must always be successful to be worthy, this might cause undue stress and fear of failure.

Promote authenticity: Once you're aware of these conditions, you can challenge them and make choices that align with your true self, rather than acting to please others or meet external standards.

Improve relationships: Understanding that conditions of worth affect not just you, but everyone can lead to more empathetic interactions with others, as you recognise the pressures they may be facing to meet their conditions of worth.

Promote self-acceptance: By letting go of unrealistic or imposed standards, you can cultivate self-acceptance, appreciating yourself for who you are rather than what you achieve.

Enhance decision-making: When you lead a self-led life, your decisions are based on your values and desires, rather than on trying to fulfill conditions of worth imposed by others.

Build resilience: Freeing yourself from these conditions can help you become more resilient to criticism and setbacks because your self-worth is not tied to external validation.

Encourage self-compassion: As you work through understanding your conditions of worth, practising self-compassion can be healing. It allows you to be kind to yourself as you navigate the complexities of reshaping your self-perception.

Using the knowledge I gained from training to be a therapist and identifying my conditions of worth helped me enhance my self-awareness, authenticity, and empathy, all of which I think are great qualities we can all develop in life. It is important that you look at your conditions as opportunities to grow. It can be both transformative and real, however you may uncover conditions that you are unable to leave behind. Seek the help of a qualified professional if you need to reach out for support with your conditions of worth.

Summary

- Conditions of worth are a natural part of life.
- Conditions we interpret as rules can affect us as we grow up.
- Through awareness, we can create change.
- Conditions may arise when we are vulnerable adults.
- Being self-led means showing compassion to yourself and others during this process.

Self-Led Life® inspired actions

- Not letting those childhood 'shoulds' drown out your adult 'wants'.
- Having compassion for self and others.
- Reaching out for support to help manage any vulnerability in later years.
- Awareness of how childhood conditions affect you as an adult.
- Recognising the importance of the effects on children and young people.

These insights will help you to identify your conditions of worth, try not to think about this too much and try to answer the questions quickly:

A reminder to use your book companion, it helps you keep everything together for reflection later.

Question 1:

Maybe some of these endings feel familiar to you. If I am to be loved I must...

- Work hard
- Not show any weakness
- Not cry
- Be quiet
- Be small
- Be clever
- Do as I am told
- Stay out of the way

Question 2: How did you learn this?

Question 3: Can you recall any particular memories?

Question 4: Have you made any decisions based on your conditions of worth?

You may have identified some conditions that are painful or make you angry. Can you take a closer look at the situation or the people who placed these conditions and try to use empathy, understanding the person was doing the best they could at the time?

If you can't find acceptance or empathy, that's ok, I hear you, find a way that works for you. I chose to create big tidal waves of change by starting with myself and then helping others, I won't ever make sense of some of the conditions or behaviours from my early years, I may not be able to change the past, but I am proud that to recognise that 'any should' that will stop me from thriving can piss off!

8
ACE - Adverse childhood experiences

TRIGGER WARNING

Before we move on to the next section, I'd like to share something that profoundly impacted me when I first learned about it. During my time at university, I learned about ACE (Adverse Childhood Experiences), which was one of those eye-opening moments for me. I couldn't believe that what I now know as common knowledge was something I had been completely unaware of before.

Your early life experiences, particularly those in childhood, greatly influence your growth, physical and mental health, and your thoughts, feelings, and behaviour. Two important aspects that affect your mental well-being are:

- The quality of your attachment relationships &
- Your experiences with Adverse Childhood Experiences (**ACEs**).

I appreciate many of you may already be aware of the concept of ACE, but for those of you who are not, I will explain the best I can. There is also plenty of information available on the internet; if you search ACE, the NHS has lots of useful resources on their website.

ACEs are Adverse Childhood Experiences. They are highly stressful and potentially traumatic events or situations that occur during childhood and/or adolescence. Toxic stress caused by Adverse Childhood Experiences (ACEs) can alter your brain development and affect the body's response to stress. ACEs have been linked to chronic health problems, mental illness, and substance abuse in adulthood. Nearly half of the people in England have experienced at least one ACE. Experiencing an ACE can reduce a person's lifespan decades after the event, and the stress can cause illness.

Understanding attachment

Attachment relates to the emotional bond you formed with your parents or caregivers from birth. This bond is essential for your development. The way your parents or caregivers respond to you helps shape your perspective on relationships. This early attachment serves as a blueprint for how you form relationships with others throughout your life, and it also influences how you view yourself and others. If you experienced positive and supportive relationships early on, you're more likely to develop a healthy view of yourself and have positive relationships in the future. Conversely, if your early caregiving experiences were less positive, for various reasons, this might lead to challenges in forming and maintaining good relationships, managing your emotions and behaviour, or feeling positive about yourself and others. When negative early attachments contribute to difficulties with relationships and mental well-being in your life, these are sometimes referred to as attachment difficulties.

There are various ACE tests that you can take to determine your score. These are available if you enter ACE Score into a search engine. *** Please make sure that any of the resources you are using are from credible sources ***

Understanding how your past can affect the present can give you a new opportunity to lead yourself into healing.

MY ACE

The lecture ended, and now an exercise appeared on the screen to complete the ACE test and discuss our score with a partner; I felt instant shame and embarrassment, and I wanted to run. Typically, this is where I would lie, I would fake the test to make it look like I had a good childhood and I'd just fly under the radar. But no, that voice inside reminded me, how could I help anyone if I wasn't able to help myself; it was another feeling that I needed to explore and another thing requiring me to dig deep. I took the paper, the questions were raw.

Did a parent or other adult in the household often or very often... Swear at you, insult you, put you down, humiliate you? or act in a way that made you afraid that you might be physically hurt? YES

Did you live with anyone who was a problem drinker or alcoholic, or who used street drugs? YES

Did you frequently or fairly often feel that ... No one in your family loved you or thought you were important or special? or Your family didn't look out for each other, feel close to each other, or support each other? YES

And so the test went on and I scored 6/10, time to discuss my score and this is where I was yet again reminded that in the courage of facing vulnerability, you get another opportunity to reconnect with yourself. My partner had a higher score than me. We managed to find some slight humour in this; we sat in the unspoken power of the fact that despite all our experiences, here we were sitting and studying for a master's degree, determined to help others.

I grappled with sharing this part with you as I didn't want to make you think that if you have experienced a lot then IT WILL impact you. But then I thought, it's common knowledge, it's on the internet and for many of you perhaps it will help you to see that you can go on to achieve great things. A high ACE score is an indicator of experiences, not destiny. The saying knowledge is power is true in this example, especially when it comes to understanding the impact of early emotional trauma on your body and brain. By acknowledging any experiences, you can take steps to oversee anything that is affecting you today.

If you, like me, have suffered several ACEs, there is a way forward, through self-awareness, you will be able to align yourself with your values and have the confidence to be your true self. I used the test score as a way of opening up to my therapist.

I don't like the idea of having a score, but it resonated with just how much my childhood environment and early relationships impacted me. I believe that some of the experiences prompted me to find and connect with myself.

Summary

- ACE are common
- ACE Can affect your attachment style
- In a 2014 UK study on ACEs, 47% of people experienced at least one ACE with 9% of the population having 4+ ACES

Self-Led Life® inspired actions

- Practise self-compassion and self-care
- Use your knowledge in the ways listed below

Here is an insight into some ways to use your knowledge.

Self-Awareness and Understanding: Recognising the specific challenges you have faced can help you gain a deeper understanding of your current behaviours, reactions, and feelings. This awareness is the first step towards positive change and personal development.

Resilience Building: People with high ACE scores often develop remarkable resilience. Use your experiences to recognise and build upon your ability to overcome challenges. This resilience can be a powerful tool in both personal and professional settings.

Empathy Towards Others: Your experiences can make you more empathetic and understanding towards others who have faced similar challenges. This empathy can be invaluable in relationships, community building, and professional roles that require interpersonal skills.

Pursuit of Healing and Personal Growth Activities: Understanding your ACE score can motivate you to seek healing, whether through therapy, support groups, or personal growth activities. Engaging in healing practises can lead to significant personal development.

Advocacy and Support: Your experiences can inspire you to advocate for others who have had similar challenges. Whether it's through volunteer work, professional roles, or informal support networks, your understanding of adversity can be a valuable asset in helping others.

Professional Insight: If your career involves working with people (such as in education, healthcare, social work, or counselling), your insights can enhance your professional skills, making you more effective in your role.

Health Awareness: A high ACE score can be associated with certain health risks. Armed with this knowledge, you can proactively manage your health with informed lifestyle choices and regular check-ups.

Mindfulness and Stress Management: Understanding the potential long-term effects of your childhood experiences can encourage you to adopt mindfulness practises and stress management techniques, which are beneficial for mental and physical health.

Personal Relationships: Your ACE score might help you understand patterns in your relationships. This insight can guide you in forming healthier relationships and improving existing ones.

Setting Boundaries: Learning about the impact of your childhood experiences can help you recognise the importance of setting healthy boundaries in all areas of your life.

9
Labels

I hope you're strapped in because I am about to get super passionate here; understanding the impact of labelling will change your life! There I said it. Labels are different to conditions of worth, labels are the quick tags we slap on people, like 'geek' or 'snob', they make it simple for us to know a lot of detail in just one name.

Are you a successful professional, a super mum, a geek, an ugly person, a 'fatty', or a loser? We often try to define ourselves by putting ourselves in certain boxes, we constantly label others and label ourselves. Here we go again... Throughout your lifetime, labels are - yes you guessed it - formed by parents, caregivers, schools, media, and friends.

The labels you have collected have shaped what you think of yourself and, behind the scenes, have influenced your thoughts and actions, whether positive or negative. They have also played a part in creating the thoughts you have about who you think you are. You may have picked up a label some time ago because of your behaviour when you were younger or certain stereotypes attached to you, such as your looks, race, sexual orientation, or illness. To be authentic it's super important that you are aware of what labels and social identities you are carrying that don't feel like they fit with who you are in this moment.

Why is it so important we know about labels?

Labels come with a judgement, either positive or negative. Typically, if a label fits with you or your surroundings, you will tend to feel good about yourself. However, if it doesn't, you may experience negative emotions such as guilt, anger, disappointment, or resentment.

One of the labels I was given when I was younger because I liked to know a lot of detail about things was OCD. It had nothing to do with the medical condition, but it was an easy and silly way for my parents to label me. This still infuriates me, to be honest, don't most children want to know what they're doing that day, how they are getting there and who they are seeing? There were quite a few labels assigned to me as I grew up; Awkward, selfish, and stuck up, they were endless in our family. The negative labels made me feel all kinds of emotions from embarrassed, or angry, to resentful. I do however also remember being called creative and still to this day, I like it, and more importantly it fits and makes me feel good.

One of the main reasons I am so passionate about spreading awareness of the wider impact negative labels is the ripple effect they can have on so many areas of your life without you realising it. Becoming more aware of the impact of labels will hopefully help you think twice before you dish one out or it's an opportunity to set a boundary if you come across someone trying to label you.

Research

Overall, the research in Labelling Theory highlights the need for careful consideration in the use of labels, particularly in sensitive areas like education and mental health, where they can have profound and lasting impacts on individuals' lives and well-being.

THE PROS AND CONS OF LABELS

Pros:

- Labels can simplify life and people, making them easier to understand and deal with.
- Labels save you time - we know who to go to for what, and who NOT to go to.

- Labels that are deemed 'positive' can make you feel secure about your identity.
- They can guide expected behaviour.
- Labels can give you permission to act in certain ways or be comfortable.

Cons:

- Labels can create limiting beliefs that hold you back, convincing you that it's just the way you are. If we believe ourselves to be forgetful or lazy, why bother trying to change?
- Often, we find ourselves trapped in difficult relationships and patterns of behaviour, often with people we have labelled.
- Labels can be limiting and inflexible, as they imply that there is only one way to behave in every situation. Even so-called positive labels, such as "kind," can lead us to prioritise others' needs over our own and make it difficult to say no.
- Labels can be a source of annoyance, frustration or anxiety as you try to live up to them or downplay them.

You're so awkward

I remember when I was around five years old, getting dressed for school, I was pulling on my long socks and felt upset when the little crinkles didn't match when I pushed them down. I remember feeling frustrated and upset that they didn't look right and I was unable to sort them out for myself.

My mum looked at me, and said, "Look at you getting all worked up over your socks! They have to be perfect, don't they? You're so awkward, Geraldine."

"Awkward" then became a label that stuck with me for what felt like an eternity. When I was nervous about going to school, I was awkward, when I wanted to become a vegetarian, I was awkward; when I didn't do things that other kids were doing, like riding roller coasters, I was awkward. I was stuck with the label; think Geri, think awkward! The problem with labels is that once you have one, people tend to focus on your behaviour specifically looking to link the label. It is as if they feel the need to prove the label right. The laser-like focus people have can stop other parts of your personality from shining through as the label takes the front and centre stage. The label of being "awkward" not only stuck, but it also affected how people perceived me. This label became part of everyday conversations where I would often hear things like, "You know what she's like, she's a bit awkward". Due to unknowingly letting this label creep into my self-belief and as an adult, I often felt awkward. The voice would pop up telling me that I was awkward and fussy if I had a different opinion or tried to set a boundary. The need to override this thought meant that often I would be overly accommodating to people or clients, which impacted some pretty big things. In the early days of running a business, I struggled to chase invoices, I would collect cash if customers didn't want to pay online, this was a huge ball ache. It didn't stop there; I overpaid my workers and even despite my HR background found it hard to discuss poor performance. Oh, and in all of that, I didn't pay myself for two years.

I had firmly and subconsciously identified with the labels that had been given to me, and eventually, they became part of who I believed I was, the labels, conditions and all the other rubbish sat in the background driving the thinking of who I was. The harm caused by labels is not in the label itself, but in the assumptions people make about the person or the thing it describes. We tend to attach certain socially-constructed thoughts or behaviours to these labels, which are often inaccurate or unfair. For example, we might assume that loud people are arrogant, rich people are educated, or certain sports people are not academic.

It is important to know that a label creates a perceived identity with a set of behaviours attached. If you were labelled a bitch there would be an assumption you would be untrustworthy, sly, cold, aggressive, and so on. Remember - it's not just about the name, but also the actions that the label represents. Take into consideration the entire impact of the label, and that it can harm our mental health.

Research shows that people who are not able to overcome the perceptions that others have about them will continue to identify themselves through their negative labels, which affects their everyday actions. So, it's super important you get a handle on any you have identified.

Through self-awareness, I started to examine some of the labels and beliefs I held, the ones that didn't sit right but also the ones that started to cause self-doubt. I even checked with a close friend who was surprised to hear that I had been labelled awkward. Of course, you can also have a positive experience with labels, as mentioned above. However, for this book, I am going to focus on the negative ones to help you have a better understanding of their impact and the power of self-awareness.

Self Labelling - A fixed sense of self

You may or may not notice, but following the lovely allocation of a label, if you have bought into it, you will also scan and eagerly collect information to support it; remember, your self-concept likes to be correct. This means you may unintentionally confirm your label by seeking out similar situations, creating a self-perpetuating cycle. When you think you can't change because of a label you've been given or given yourself, you will start to assume that you can't do certain things. Your day-to-day becomes more stressful if you're trying to negotiate your way through it by avoiding tasks you 'can't' do.

Labels can sometimes limit your sense of identity because they can become too rigid. While labels such as mother, friend, professional, student, or religious may align with our values, we can become too attached to them and value ourselves solely based on these labels.

To get to the true self it's important to keep a balanced perspective and not allow labels to define your entire identity. For example, being a mother is important to me, but if I over-identify as a mum it could lead to self-criticism for every parenting failure. I would have the unhelpful laser beam 'mum' focus on myself, judging my actions and behaviours through that 'mum' lens. Pressuring myself to do what 'normal' mums do etc.

When you hold rigid expectations for how you should appear and act, you will lack compassion for yourself and can limit your potential for authentic growth. You will create unrealistic expectations of yourself which can lead to feelings of inadequacy and discouragement when you fail to meet the expectations of the label.

Labels can become addictive

When considering the instinctive drive to protect your self-concept, it makes sense that people often subconsciously use labels as a shield to protect themselves. However, the labels can also create a divide between how others perceive us and our true selves. Sometimes, living up to a label allows us to take a break from the pressures of the outside world.

For example, Amy has a medical condition that has become the focal point of her identity. Although it affects her ability to participate in certain activities and energy levels. Her health condition is not life-threatening or deemed as serious. The label of the condition plays a significant role in her everyday life and interaction with others. She may restrict her social interactions preferring to stay at home, and her friends may not consider inviting her to places. Although there are lots of things to be considered, the label does not define Amy's true identity, she could restrict the opportunity for personal growth by limiting her chances of trying new things that could help her condition. By conforming to the label, Amy neglects her true self and hides her skills and abilities. It seems that she cannot distinguish herself from the label and has become used to the distance it creates between her and her identity.

Desperate to prove the label wrong

It's possible that you can become fixated on not being a label that was given to you. I can also relate to this one and have seen many people try to get as far away from the labels as possible! Let's say someone labels you as a failure; then you may spend your focus on working hard to prove 'others wrong'. Pay attention, as in the process of rebelling against an unwanted identity, you may have lost touch with your true self.

Andy grew up in a poor household and was teased at school and labelled the poor smelly kid.

A label that understandably he was desperate to get away from and so he spent years throwing himself into his career in sales. He travelled the world and at work was regularly promoted, he became obsessed with sports cars, houses, and living a luxury lifestyle. The more money he earned, the more things he would buy and the further away the poor label became. Despite thinking that all those things made him happy on the surface, his main aim in life was to prove others wrong, had he missed the chance to really discover what made him happy?

Sometimes the powerful labels we try to escape can propel us with that much force we don't see what we're missing. A chance to work in a job that brings you more fulfilment. To find a soul mate or start a family or not?

To become the person you aspire to be, it's essential to understand that the labels you attach to yourself play an important role in this journey. You can choose not to allow these labels to limit your future path and not let them hold you back. My hope is that we can all be more mindful of the impact, words, actions labels have on a person's self-esteem.

Research

There is a lot of research to support the negative impact of labelling children and people in general. As Brown explained, there is usually a 'downward mobility' once a label is attached to a person. I want to draw your attention to the moments when you feel the need to label someone and how it can lead to a fixed identity and a set of beliefs that may pull the person away from their true self.

Children and labels

If you have used labels to define or categorise children or other people in the past and now feel guilty about it, be kind to yourself; we all do it! As you work on creating a self-led version of yourself, you will become more aware on the impact of labels and the importance of promoting curiosity and self-acceptance.

Let us look at how easy it happens: Ryan was at a gymnastics show. He laughed with another parent as the children got ready for the annual performance. He said, “Sally will have no problems with this, she's so sassy.” How many times do you hear this, or have you said it, I know I have! But based on what we now know, can you make sense of what can happen from here? The label has been given, the laser beam focus is on. Ryan mentions 'she is also this sassy in school' of course she is! Friends and family, perhaps even her teacher know her as 'sassy Sally' and will all be watching out for signs of 'sass'. It's now highly likely, little Sally will act in ways that are stereotypically associated with ‘sassy’.

Understanding the importance of labelling can help you establish healthy relationships, maintain boundaries, and avoid negative connections. It can also help you to teach others and create change, keeping in mind the wider impact of 'just a label'. Practice self-care and compassion, and remember the power you hold in choosing to remove old labels.

If you fancy more learning or a more detailed exploration, Howard Becker's book “Outsiders: Studies in the Sociology of Deviance” gives a detailed understanding of labelling theory.

Summary

- We all do it, be kind to yourself and learn.
- Labels are everywhere, this is about awareness.
- They can happen in kindness and innocence.
- We love them because they are easy for our brains, one word sets the scene.
- You and others will search for behaviours confirming the label, making it feel even more real.
- Having a label can result in 'downward mobility' and affect how you feel about yourself.

Self-Led Life® Inspired actions

Self-Reflection and Awareness: This involves recognising how labels and stereotypes might have shaped your own beliefs and behaviours. You reflect on your own experiences and biases, and consider how they have influenced your perceptions of yourself and others.

Critical Thinking: You critically evaluate the labels and stereotypes you encounter, questioning their validity and origin. This means not accepting stereotypes or labels at face value and understanding that they are often oversimplifications.

Empathy and Understanding: You strive to understand the perspectives and experiences of others who may be affected by labelling. This involves listening to their experiences and recognising the impact that labels can have on individuals' mental health and social interactions.

Challenging Labels and Stereotypes: When you recognise harmful labels or stereotypes, whether in yourself or your environment, you take steps to challenge and change them.

Promoting Inclusivity and Respect: You actively promote an inclusive and respectful environment where individuals are seen as more than just labels or stereotypes. This involves encouraging others to see the unique qualities and experiences of each person.

Personal Growth: You commit to ongoing learning and personal growth, understanding that awareness of the negative effects of labelling is a continuous process. You stay open to new information and perspectives that might challenge your existing beliefs.

Mindfulness and Emotional Regulation: You practise mindfulness and emotional regulation to manage your reactions to labels and stereotypes. This helps in responding thoughtfully rather than reacting impulsively when confronted with labelling situations.

Modelling Positive Behaviour: You lead by example,

showing others how to interact respectfully and without reliance on harmful labels or stereotypes.

Being self-led is about taking responsibility for your thoughts and actions, and actively working towards a more understanding and less judgemental approach to yourself and others. It's a proactive stance against the oversimplification and harm that can come from careless labelling.

These insights will help you to think about some of the labels you were given.

A reminder to use the book companion!

- What are some of the labels you give yourself? Fat, strong, weak, clever, dumb, aim for at least four or five.
- Decide if each label is 'positive' or 'negative'.
- Get digging, where did it come from? For instance, it could be from society, such as TV, books, and magazines, or people, such as our parents, peers, friends, or teachers.
- Be as specific as possible and ask yourself if you agree with the label.
- What advantages and disadvantages does each label have?
- Has labelling affected your life?

- Do the labels help or hinder you, and in what ways do they limit you?
- What goals in my life is this label getting in the way of me achieving?
- Is there anything that contradicts your label? For example, if you consider yourself antisocial, have you ever displayed outgoing behaviour which suggests different?
- Which labels would you like to keep – and which would you like to lose?
- What labels are you giving to others around you that could negatively or positively impact their life?
- Review your list of your labels; which ones are you keeping and which ones are going?

10

How were you set free?

I hope you have enjoyed the first part of the book where you have hopefully had some valuable insights into what may have impacted who you THINK you are.

Take time to reflect on all you have learned through the exercises and the lightbulb moments, you have had. I hope you have a deeper understanding of how your beliefs shape you and recognise the power within to change who you THINK you are. Bringing all of your many experiences and beliefs together you may wonder how they have influenced you and perhaps what decisions you have gone on to make as a result. To help you reflect on your own experience, I want to share with you another significant part of my journey, *how I was set free.*

As I reflected on the information I had collected about myself, the conditions, beliefs and labels, I began bringing it all together. I started to think about my younger self, how I felt about myself at the time of leaving home and how it went on to impact my choices and thinking over the years, see if you can think of how you were set free.

I was sixteen when I left home; it's in my awareness, looking back at age forty-four, that I see just how the early home environment impacted the rest of my adolescent journey and up to my early thirties.

It has been through expanding my self-awareness that I have been able to turn the direction of my travels. This has been one of my most significant lightbulb moments, being able to look back and piece it all together to understand what drove my decisions to make sure they were not about to dictate the rest of my journey. Just like when you put a destination in a sat nav, it looks at your current location so it can decide the best route to take you on. It has to know the starting point just like you do.

At what point in your life did you become an independent thinker? What beliefs did you take with you when you left home?

As a teenager, found it very embarrassing having functional alcoholic parents, this was one of the many reasons I couldn't wait to leave home. I always knew it wasn't safe, and I always felt on edge.

Let's pretend for a moment when we leave our family home or get to an age where we are independent thinkers, we are handed a big box. Inside the box is everything our parents or caregivers are handing over to us, it contains all the information that has built our life to date. The conditions of worth, what we like, what we don't like, and they hand it to you so you can take it from there, much like a handover you would put together in work before taking annual leave.

What's in the box?

Let us pretend I was handed my box at the front door of my family home as I was leaving to start my life as an independent lady of the world age sixteen. What was in my box? What tools did I have? What things would help me?

My box was full of fear, shame, abandonment, rage, and more shame. Inside the handover notes were blank, there had been nothing to add. I was impressionable, vulnerable, and left to my own devices. When I entered the big wide world, I had a lot of challenges to deal with, but I remember in fondness my unshakable instinct to survive and thrive despite those early circumstances.

The contents in my box dictated the career path I

chose, propelled by anxiety and shame, I wanted to earn money, be taken seriously and be somebody. I wanted to blast off as far away from those labels as I could. My feelings about myself also reflected in how I behaved at times, certainly during my teenage years. Looking back, I can see why I eventually ended up working in Human Resources and senior management roles, I see they kept me safe. Both from a financial point of view, but also the hidden belief that being a manager meant I was less likely to be judged and more likely to be seen and taken seriously. This makes sense now, remember those conditions that forced me to grow up fast in order to have a seat at that adult table? Did I choose the career I wanted or one that helped me survive the big world, one that would mean I could use my learned survival skills which meant I thrived in faced-paced environments and was a stickler for the detail?

Theme?

I see this a lot; people end up in careers that keep them safe by doing what they know. I see therapists and nurses who used to be carers for families, and I see people working on their own due to trust issues. It makes sense that we choose familiar things as the brain likes to keep us safe and will use our previous experiences to inform the choices we make about our future.

Was it always there?

I question, what career would I have chosen if I hadn't been fuelled by fear and labels for all those years and had a little more self-awareness. I know... I would be an author!

At age nine in primary school, I loved creative writing. Enid Blyton and Roald Dahl were my heroes, like many children those books helped me to escape into magical places. I remember one day in school we were asked to write a story, I cannot remember all of the details, but I do remember my teacher Mr Lyons (he was such an amazing teacher) asked us to write a story. I remember how I felt writing it, I was excited, time seemed to disappear, and I felt connected and happy. Coupled with the space that allowed me to 'dare to dream' it was magical. I knew back then I wanted to write or be creative.

As you may relate, being busy with life and all the other stuff we often don't get a chance to lean into those glimmers (opposite to triggers). We are swept away from one event and activity to the next with an overload of information. It is so important that, like any good teacher, we give children the courage to lean into what lights them up.

I do believe that the creative glimmer never left me, it tried to come out in various creative ways over the years and eventually, I think my dream came knocking again when I 'cracked open' and this time I had to listen.

When you know you know

The very moment I went to Keele University I felt like I was home, it's more a feeling than words. The same happened when I loaned a horse, the feeling I got when I was shovelling poo and brushing his hair was again indescribable, I just knew it was something I needed at the time to help me heal. Animals are often the go-to when people are feeling anxious or suffering with poor mental health, I believe it's because we are craving those non-judgemental, compassionate connections to soothe us.

You will find out where you are meant to be by putting yourself there and leaning into it if you like it. If you're curious about a new hobby like art or a sport, go watch a class. If you want to change career, go link in with someone who's in the job, visit the office. Once you're in the environment that's meant for you, you will know. You have to go and see what it feels like, it's these moments where there are no words you just have to go and see, trust me when you know you know.

Reflecting on all of the many things we explored that I had inherited as part of my childhood helped me to see how I was propelled into adulthood. By looking at how I was set free I was able to see that I had not had a chance to lean into my glimmers as I was busy surviving. When I 'cracked open' it gave me a chance to reclaim my identity and reset.

This final insight will help you uncover what was in your box and how it has affected your journey so far. Have you, like me, missed any moments to connect with your true self, were there glimmers hijacked by the instinct to survive? There is a great part dedicated to this in - you guessed it.... The book companion, visit **gericarey.com**.

What was in your box?

What was in your box, and has it influenced your journey? Recalling the positives and negatives let's look at your journey.

- What age were you?
- What labels have made it into the box?
- What beliefs have made it into the box?
- What was the primary emotion that propelled you into the world?
- What was your first job? Are there any connections?
- What decisions did you go on to make as a result?
- Did it affect your choices in career or partner(s)?
- How do you feel about your box?

Part 2

Welcome to the second part of the book, here, I share some of my most valuable teachings from the world of Psychology and Psychotherapy. This part has a series of mini masterclasses that you can use to help you navigate any areas of growth that you have identified or any crossroads that you may encounter along the way. These are short, jam-packed, bite-size learnings that can be completed using the book companion.

11
Parent, Adult, Child - You can choose

As a way of exploring your communication I would love to introduce to you the Parent-Adult-Child model, which can be really effective in identifying where communication failures can happen and why.

The Parent Adult Child (PAC) Model will help you to understand more clearly what is taking place between two people in a situation, as well as to help you understand yourself and your own reactions. When you have awareness and understanding of your own parent, adult and child you are able to choose which ego state to adopt, which helps you to make the most of your communication and create and maintain better relationships.

The Parent Adult Child Model (PAC) is a part of Transactional Analysis theory. Eric Berne was an

American medical doctor and trained psychiatrist, who, was interested in discovering ways of making psychoanalysis more accessible to ordinary people. He believed that each of us have 3 ego states (our **Parent**, **Adult** and **Child**) it is important to note that the terms parent, adult and child have a slightly different meaning within the background of the theory than they do in normal, day to day language:

Three Egos

Parent: This is like your inner voice that is copied from your parents or authority figures. It can be nurturing and protective, but sometimes it's critical and controlling. It's like when you hear a voice in your head saying, 'You should do this,' or 'Don't do that!' Parent can also be described as an ego state that is **TAUGHT.**

Adult: This is your rational self. It is all about being in the here and now, dealing with facts and logic. It is that cool, calm, and collected part of you that looks at things objectively and makes decisions based on reality. In addition, the Adult in you helps keep your Parent and Child in check.

Child: This is the ego state in which you behave, feel and think similarly to how you did as a child. For example, if your boss gives you some negative feedback you may react by looking at the floor, or crying, or getting angry. The Child ego is your expression of feelings, thoughts and emotions that are being replayed from childhood. The Child ego state has two main parts, It is spontaneous, emotional, and creative, but it can also be scared or rebellious. Think about moments when you feel free or times when you're scared and just want some comfort. Child can also be described as an ego state that is **FELT.**

Waking the child

If you talk to someone in Critical Parent mode, you will risk waking up the rebellious child in the other person. So a parent saying 'You didn't pass that test? Are you stupid?' is going to be feel like a punch in the gut for a child who just wants a 'Well Done'. As an adult, if you say to your partner something like 'I see you couldn't be bothered to take the bins out', you are talking like a Critical Parent.

BUT in doing so you risk a rebellious child reaction, which could potentially lead to an intense disagreement.

I can imagine you have had people speak to you like Critical Parents. You may agree with them at the time, but inside you were thinking something totally different. Critical parents often display nonverbal cues of frustration or annoyance, like pointing fingers, clenching fists, or invading personal space.

Have you ever heard someone sounding like their parent and told them, “You sound just like your mum/dad,” this happens because they're adapting the tone of a 'critical parent'.

In Child mode, your emotional response is heightened, and it can manifest in various ways like sadness, anger, worry, fear, or low spirits. You might also adopt childlike gestures such as fidgeting, laughing nervously, whimpering, or giving noncommittal responses. Often, you'll find yourself using straightforward, direct phrases characteristic of a child, like “I want,” “I need,” “I don't care,” or “I don't know.”

For example, consider how an adult might act when receiving disappointing news. They might slump their shoulders, let out a sigh, and use simple expressions of unhappiness, like “This isn't fair,” or “Why does this always happen to me?” These reactions are seeking empathy or understanding, akin to how a child looks for comfort from a nurturing figure.

Similarly, children often naturally display these behaviours in various settings, whether they’re seeking attention, care, or sympathy. They might use a certain tone, gesture, or phrase that instinctively prompts an adult's nurturing response. Have you ever observed how a child might exaggerate a pout or use a particularly whiny voice to get a parent's attention? They're relying on a universal cue for nurturing, hoping to engage the 'Nurturing Parent' in the adult they're addressing.

Unsurprisingly if you behave like a child, you may trigger a critical response from those around you, which can be detrimental to your self-esteem.

How can you manage this?

Be self-led, be aware of how you are communicating and how people are responding to you, choose the adult to represent you in the right circumstances, you will transform the way you interact with others and manage situations. Being self-led is essentially about taking charge of your actions and emotions. This means leading yourself with the composure and responsibility expected of an adult. You maintain an upright posture, showing confidence and willingness to engage constructively. Eye contact is crucial—it shows honesty and a willingness to connect on a deeper level.

In conversation, a self-led person speaks with a firm yet moderate tone. This approach ensures that your words are taken seriously without being overbearing. It's about expressing your thoughts and opinions with conviction while respecting the right of others to do the same. Assertiveness is key here; it's the golden mean between passivity and aggression. By advocating for yourself respectfully, you encourage others to do the same.

Avoiding emotionally charged language is another aspect of being self-led. It means you choose clarity and logic over words that can escalate tensions. This disciplined way of communicating can prevent misunderstandings and facilitate a calm resolution to potential conflicts.

The lightbulb moment comes when you recognise these states not just in yourself, but in others, and adjust your communication accordingly.

Applying the PAC model in your life means you start to listen not just to the words, but also to the 'who' in the conversation. Is the 'Parent' criticizing? Is the 'Adult' reasoning? Is the 'Child' reacting? With this awareness, you can choose a more effective 'role' to engage with, leading to clearer, more understanding, and more positive interactions in every area of your life.

Summary

- Three Ego states Parent, the Adult, and the Child.
- Helps you understand your relationships and communication better.
- The goal with PAC is to strengthen your adult part.
- It is about recognising who's in charge and checking in.

Self-Led Life® inspired actions

- Find your power in being able to choose to move towards an adult role.
- Understand people on a new level and meet them with compassion.
- Think about who is representing you and how you are reacting.
- Use this in all areas of your life to help when communicating with others.

Here's a set of questions and a simple exercise to you identify which state you are operating from and how to apply this knowledge in your life.

Questions to Identify Your PAC State

1. When faced with a challenge, do you find yourself seeking approval or instructions from others, as a child might (Child state)?
2. Do you often find yourself critical or nurturing towards others, as a parent would be (Parent state)?
3. How frequently do you approach situations logically and objectively, focusing on the here and now (Adult state)?

Exercise to Apply PAC in Daily Life

Step 1: Self-Observation

For one week, take note of moments when you feel particularly emotional or reactive. What was happening, and how did you respond?

Step 2: Identify the State

Reflect on each noted incident and identify whether your reaction was from the Parent, Adult, or Child state. Ask yourself:

- Was I seeking guidance or approval? (Child)
- Was I trying to guide or judge someone? (Parent)

Step 3: Evaluate the Outcome

Consider whether the state you were in was helpful or if another state would have led to a better outcome.

Step 4: Practice Shifting States

Next time you recognise you're in the Parent or Child state, consciously try to shift to the Adult state. For example, if you're feeling overly critical (Parent state), attempt to assess the situation dispassionately (Adult state).

Step 5: Reflection

At the end of the week, reflect on the changes in your interactions when applying the PAC model. Did operating from the Adult state change the outcomes?

By routinely practicing this exercise, you can begin to increase your self-awareness and improve interactions with others.

Understanding PAC isn't about judging yourself or others, it's about leading yourself in recognising the power over your reactions and interactions with others. If you are interested in this therapeutic approach, ask a professional therapist who is trained in Transactional Analysis.

12
Deepening Your Journey of Self-Acceptance

Following the expansion of your self-awareness, the next important part of your learning is to include self-acceptance. This can be the learning that is often left to catch up, if you don't make time to focus on accepting yourself you won't have the foundations you need for growth. Learning how to accept yourself on a deeper level will help make your life flow naturally. As you learn to love and accept where you are now, you will have the courage to continue the journey to your true self.

Self-acceptance is the brave journey of embracing every part of who you are, including the chapters written in the shadows. Carl Rogers' profound insight into self-acceptance laid a foundation for personal growth and well-being. We all make mistakes; we are human. Self-acceptance forgives the actions and decisions made in your past, particularly under challenging circumstances.

Sometimes we try and run away from mistakes by changing aspects of ourselves or hiding away, I do wonder how this affects us on a deeper level.

Self-acceptance is a multidimensional idea. It's complex, it involves recognising and embracing your strengths, acknowledging, and learning from your weaknesses, and being compassionate towards your past self, who navigated life's challenges as best as they could.

Being surrounded by addiction all of my life the main thing I notice is the impact of the shame around the things that have happened in the past. The dance I see all too often is how the shadows of the past effect the actions and decisions we take towards the future. I want to dedicate this mini-learning to those of you who want to explore shame and a way of accepting past mistakes to help you move you towards living a better life.

Positive Self Regard

As you bring together all of your learnings it's important that you start to build the foundations to support yourself. A huge part of the journey will require you to visit your self-esteem. To reach where you want to go, you have to be able to accept yourself. I don't mean anything cheesy here, but in honesty, if you can't look in a mirror or struggle to accept compliments, there's a little work to do. The way I knew I needed to work on my self-esteem was simple... I looked in the mirror and I didn't like what I saw. I knew that there was absolutely no point in continuing to plaster over the fact that I was avoiding the person that was going to achieve all of the great things I had planned. I had to dig deep and turn my focus on healing the inside, otherwise the same old cycles of being stuck would repeat. Positive self-regard is as important as the goals you set, how can you reach them if you're not leading yourself to check in on your self-esteem? That doesn't mean you have to change anything overnight, remember it's about the awareness here. Notice that you're having a hard time with your esteem, making sure your goals are aligned and you're practising self-compassion.

Positive self-regard is the ability to access and value yourself unconditionally. It means having a basic level of self-respect and a positive self-image, regardless of external validation, criticism, or failure.

According to Rogers, this is not just about feeling good about yourself it's about appreciating yourself without conditions or requirements. It allows you to embrace your authentic experiences and feelings without fear of judgement. When you regard yourself positively, you're more inclined to trust your own decisions and feelings, which is essential for personal growth and self-actualisation - the realisation of your full potential.

How positive regard affects personal growth

Positive regard is linked to resilience and psychological well-being, it enables you to better handle setbacks and challenges, reminding you that your worth is not based on success or the approval of others. This self-compassion creates an environment where you can take risks, make mistakes, and learn from them, all of which are an essential part of the personal development journey.

The origin of self-regard

According to Rogers, positive self-esteem is developed in early childhood. Children who receive unconditional love and acceptance from their caregivers learn to accept themselves as they are. On the other hand, those who receive love and approval only when they meet certain conditions as we have learned may tend to feel worthy only when they fulfil those expectations, this kind of love and approval is what Rogers called *conditional positive regard.*

How to develop self-regard

- Practising self-acceptance and self-compassion.

- Recognising and challenging conditions you've placed on your worth.
- Surrounding yourself with positive relationships that offer unconditional positive regard.
- Encouraging others to become aware of the importance of self-esteem.

Challenges to positive self-regard

Many people struggle with maintaining positive self-regard due to societal pressures and internalised conditions of worth. It is normal to feel inadequate when comparing yourself to others or the standards set by the society you live in. However, recognising that these external conditions are a powerful and essential part of leading a Self-Led Life®, you can recognise the source of the problem and take action. If you notice that someone's social media is affecting how you feel about yourself then make a choice, and look at the bigger picture, the effect on your self-esteem will impact the journey to your future self!

Embracing positive self-regard

Here are some of the things you can do to help you tap into your inner self-acceptance, you may have already completed a few of them as part of the earlier learning, but I always find it helpful to share different approaches to help broaden the tools you have available and find the things that work for you.

Unconditional self-acceptance letter

Write a letter to yourself expressing unconditional love and acceptance. Acknowledge your strengths as well as your weaknesses, affirming that your worth is not dependent on perfection. Pledge to support yourself in moments of doubt just as you would support a dear friend. You could try writing to your younger self as a mother figure, what would you say? How would you comfort them?

Two chairs dialogue

This exercise, although it may sound strange, just like talking out loud, really can help you externalise and address negative self-talk with compassion. It is what is known as 'chair work'. Set up two chairs facing each other. In one chair sit as your 'critical self' and voice all of your self-criticisms. Then, switch to the other chair as your 'compassionate self' and respond to each criticism with understanding and acceptance. If this doesn’t 'sit' right with you, pardon the pun, then you can also do this by writing letters. You can respond with the more compassionate voice, which is how I found my OWL!

Self-acceptance meditation

Listen to a guided meditation that's focussed on self-acceptance. Visualise your successes and failures, your happiness and pain, and envelop all of those experiences in a warm accepting light. Use affirmations such as 'I accept myself wholly and completely'.

The mirror exercise

Can you stand in front of a mirror, look at yourself in the eyes and say something positive? This can be extremely challenging if you are used to self-criticism, take this slowly it's a powerful way of building a relationship with yourself that is based on kindness and acceptance.

Exploring values

Identify your core values through journaling or a values card exercise. Check out gericarey.com for all book resources. Reflect on how your life aligns with your chosen values. Recognising and living in line with your values is an important step in developing positive self-regard.

Conditions of worth inventory

Return to the list of conditions that you made note of earlier in the book, the ones you believe you must meet to earn acceptance from yourself and others. Write a counter statement next to your conditions affirming that you are worthy of love and respect regardless of what those conditions are.

Self-compassion breaks

Whenever you notice you're being hard on yourself, take time to make sure you practise self-compassion fiercely or in your own way.

Gratitude for self

Each night write down three things you are grateful for about yourself. These can be qualities, actions you took or simply parts of your character you have appreciated that day.

Role model visualisation

Visualise a person who has positive regard, someone who values and respects themselves. Imagine them speaking to you in a loving and accepting manner and try to adopt this tone when you speak to yourself. This can be a really handy and fun thing to do, you can ask yourself things like, 'What would Oprah say'? You will be surprised by how it can help reframe your thinking.

Practising positive self-regard in the same way can help you to build a strong relationship with yourself. It means that you believe you have the inner resources to find their way forward and extend respect to yourself.

In therapy, we refer to UPR - Unconditional Positive Regard. It is the basic acceptance and support of a person regardless of what they say or do, especially in the context of client-centred therapy. It is one of the conditions that help create the environment that aids a client to change. As you can imagine, it's a really important part of the therapeutic relationship. It is through experiencing the power, the effects of UPR have with clients and experiencing it in therapy myself, that I see the value of practicing unconditional positive regard in everyday life. It is the ability to see another person as doing the best they can in the circumstances they are in. You can practice UPR with others by putting your personal opinion to one side and receive and accept them just the way they are.

> "People are just as wonderful as sunsets if you let them be. When I look at a sunset, I don't find myself saying, 'Soften the orange a bit on the right-hand corner.' I don't try to control a sunset. I watch with awe as it unfolds."
>
> — Carl Rogers

13
Courage to be vulnerable and the fear of being seen

Vulnerability is a word that often comes with a lot of judgement, being aware of when you feel most vulnerable and how it affects you in the rawest of moments, will help you and encourage others to do the same.

As you lead yourself to your authentic self, you are going to feel vulnerable, it's normal you will be leaning into things that perhaps have not been allowed or you were judged for. I suffer from the fear of being seen and judged by others, this is where a lot of my own vulnerability comes from and the biggest thing I continue to work on. (For this part I am focused on the judgement we receive from the outside critics not how we judge ourselves).

How have I written this book then? As I sit writing this chapter, I want to share that I am still scared and anxious, but my why and the reason I am continuing to type is that power inside that tells me to dare greatly.

I don't have an entourage who are willing me to do this. In fact, in the process of writing a book-changing career and making some radical personal upgrades I have lost touch with people along the way.

It is a natural part of growth; As we have learned, we all are unique and have our individual circumstances. It is easy to assume that the people you don't see very often or are separated from will judge you, and that's ok. Judgement is going to show up no matter what you do; it's a natural part of life. Some people will judge you more than others and opinions will change over time, we're all human.

To help me deal with these moments I think of this precious one chance we all get at life, what's the worst that can happen, I have seen far too many people leave this earth too soon. I draw strength from thinking about my little beautiful family and making them proud.

I have no idea what will happen in writing this book, I hope it helps you and I hope it helps me to spread the message about the great things we can achieve by starting with understanding who you really are. My fear of being seen runs deep, I must venture this new self-awareness alone, standing in my power and choosing to lean into the love of those I have close to me. I reflect on the people I have helped and the lives that can be changed by bringing this next level of self-awareness to others. Helping to create changes that start from the inside of each one of us.

A message to your outside critics

As well as the inner critic, you may find some people who are critical of the changes you are making, or you might imagine what they are saying about you.

I have seen the fear of judgement from others stop many people from doing the things that they feel destined for and losing out on the chance to be happier.

We can and will find the courage to stand and fight, for each other, we will continue to show up and continue to grow. I hope the critics out there will see any feelings of judgement as an invitation to get curious. I hope they find the self-compassion to look within and the courage to uncover their authenticity in all of its glory.

To help manage the thoughts I have about the critics, I read Daring Greatly by Brene Brown and I still regularly watch her Ted Talks. It was when I was watching the talk she gave about the inner critic I experienced a little glimmer (opposite of trigger). I felt the unwavering confidence that I was able to stand up in my power and speak. It was only the fear of judgement stopping me in my tracks.

As per Theodore Roosevelt's famous speech, 'Vulnerability is the celebration of the courage and effort over criticism'. To lead yourself, you must dare greatly and be able to tap into your inner knowing (Your Owl) and ignore the judgements.

Man in the Arena - I have these words framed at home, it's a powerful reminder - have the confidence to try. I have given it a little upgrade and changed to 'Person in the Arena'.

Person in the arena

'It is not the critic who counts; not the man who points out how the strong man stumbles, or where the doer of deeds could have done them better. The credit belongs to the person who is actually in the arena, whose face is marred by dust and sweat and blood; who strives valiantly; who errs, who comes short again and again, because there is no effort without error and shortcoming; but who does actually strive to do the deeds; who knows great enthusiasms, the great devotions; who spends themself in a worthy cause; who at the best knows in the end the

triumph of high achievement, and who at the worst, if they fail, at least fails while daring greatly, so that their place shall never be with those cold and timid souls who neither know victory nor defeat.' - Theodore Roosevelt

When you are uncovering your authentic self, you need to get behind many layers which have been hidden and never seen before. You will feel vulnerable because it's new! That is all it is. In this 'newness' you will start to create a new way of being that will in time become your new ' normal'.

Summary

- Vulnerability is a part of growth and change.
- Judgement is often an automatic response based on personal beliefs.

Self-Led Life® inspired actions

- Finding the courage to find your way of handling external critics.
- Lead by example.
- Practice self-compassion and compassion for others.

Vulnerability in the face of judgement

This insight will help guide you through a process of self-reflection, helping you to recognise and embrace moments of vulnerability in the face of judgement.

Identify a moment of judgement

Reflect on a situation where you felt judged by others; it might have been a comment from a friend a family gathering, a situation at work or even an internal judgement you've placed on yourself.

How did you feel?

Write about the emotions you experienced during this moment. Were you hurt, angry, embarrassed, or perhaps indifferent? Describe your thoughts and any physical sensations you felt.

How did you react?

Reflect on how you reacted to the judgement. Did you close off, defend yourself or perhaps show vulnerability? Was this reflection effective and align with how you wish to handle judgement in the future?

Any lessons?

Reflect on what this experience has taught you. how did facing judgement and showing vulnerability contribute to your personal growth? What insights did you gain about yourself and how you relate to others?

Think about how you would prefer to handle similar situations going forward. What actions can you take to respond with more courage and openness even in the face of judgement?

Pop this where you can see it!

'I am capable of facing judgement with courage and openness, my vulnerability is a strength that leads me to growth and authentic connections.'

14
Judgement and the JUDGE Method

Think about the last time you made a judgement about someone or even yourself. Was it today, an hour ago, or just a few moments back? You might not realise it, but you make judgements every day. These judgements, large and small, shape how you see the world, interact with people, and view yourself.

But have you ever stopped to wonder why you judge? Often, it's your insecurities, fears, or a deep-seated need to make sense of the complexities around you that drive these judgements. It is natural to judge; it's part of being human. However, when left unchecked, your judgements can create misunderstandings, strain your relationships, and feed an inner critic that chips away at your self-esteem.

In this chapter, inspired by Gabrielle Bernstein's transformative approach in "Judgement Detox," I'll help you to understand and alleviate your judgemental habits. Think of this as a detox for your tendency to judge, a way to cleanse your perspectives and interactions.

The aim isn't to completely eradicate judgement—that's not just unrealistic, but also impossible. Rather, this journey is about gaining awareness, understanding the roots of your judgements, and gradually replacing harsh judgements with compassion and empathy, both towards yourself and others. By engaging in this process, you're taking a significant step towards a more peaceful, empathetic, and fulfilling life.

How do you judge?

Notice how often you judge yourself. Maybe it's when you look in the mirror, or when you make a mistake at work. These moments, when you're critical of your actions or appearance, are instances of self-judgement. It is that internal voice that's constantly evaluating you, often harshly. This self-judgement can affect how you feel about yourself, leading to lowered self-esteem or even anxiety. It's important to recognise when this happens because the way you talk to yourself matters. Ask yourself, "Would I talk to a friend the way I talk to myself?"

When you judge others

Now, think about the times you form opinions about others. Maybe it's a snap judgement about someone based on their appearance or a quick conclusion about their character from a brief interaction. This kind of judgement might seem harmless, but it can shape your interactions and relationships. When you judge others, you're seeing them through a lens coloured by your own biases and experiences. Remember, each person has their own story, and your judgements can prevent you from seeing the true depth of their character.

Why do you do it?

Take a moment to reflect on why you judge. It's not just a simple habit; there are deeper reasons behind it.

How have your past experiences shaped your judgements? Every interaction, every relationship, every triumph, and every setback you've experienced plays a role in how you perceive and judge the world. These experiences, especially those from your younger years, often set the foundation for your judgement patterns. For instance, if you've been criticised heavily in the past, you might find yourself more critical of others or yourself.

Now, think about the influences from society around you. The culture you grew up in, the values your community holds, the media you consume - all these things contribute to your judgement framework. Society often dictates norms and expectations, subtly influencing how you perceive what's 'right' or 'wrong', 'acceptable' or 'unacceptable'.

What about any personal insecurities? Judgement can be a shield, a way to protect yourself from your vulnerabilities. By judging others, you might be deflecting attention from your flaws or using it as a mechanism to feel in control. Similarly, self-judgement often stems from not feeling good enough, a reflection of your deepest insecurities and fears.

Understanding these roots is not about assigning blame but about gaining clarity. By acknowledging and examining these influences, you empower yourself to start transforming how you judge.

The Healing Touch of Self-Compassion

Think about a recent situation where you were hard on yourself. Maybe you made a mistake at work, had an argument with a friend, or failed to meet a personal goal. How did you react? Were you critical and harsh, or did you offer yourself understanding and patience? Embracing self-compassion means allowing yourself to be human, to be flawed, and to learn from your experiences without harsh self-judgement. When you practise self-compassion, you create a safe space for growth and healing.

Encouraging Empathy

Your journey of understanding judgement doesn't stop with yourself. It extends to how you perceive and interact with others. Empathy is your bridge to understanding the feelings and perspectives of people around you. It's about putting yourself in their shoes and seeing the world from their viewpoint. Think about a recent time when you judged someone else. What led to that judgement? Was it a lack of understanding, a quick assumption, or a reaction based on your own biases? Now, reimagine that situation with empathy. Consider what that person might have been going through, their challenges, fears, and hopes. Understanding others' circumstances can significantly reduce the tendency to judge and can foster deeper connections and a more compassionate view of the world around you.

Acceptance and Positive Regard

Close your eyes for a moment and think again about a recent situation where you found yourself judging either yourself or someone else. Now, reimagine that scenario, but this time, approach it with acceptance. Acceptance doesn't mean agreeing with or condoning every action or thought. Instead, it's about acknowledging and understanding these thoughts and actions without harsh judgement.

When you embrace acceptance towards yourself, you're saying, “It's okay to be imperfect. It's okay to make mistakes.” This mindset shift is powerful. It allows you to view your actions and thoughts as they are, not as you think they should be. This shift from a critical to an accepting mindset can help reduce any internal conflict and help create inner peace.

Non-Judgemental Attitude in Daily Life

Imagine going through your day without judging the people you meet or interact with. This doesn't mean you won't have opinions or reactions, but it does mean you'll hold these opinions lightly, without letting them define or limit your understanding of others.

Start by noticing when you make snap judgements about others. Ask yourself, “What's behind this judgement? Is it truly reflective of the person, or is it more about my perceptions and biases?”

The Power of Understanding in Building Connections

Understanding is the bridge between judgement and acceptance. It involves putting yourself in someone else's shoes trying to see the world from their perspective. When you understand where someone is coming from, their actions and words make more sense. This understanding can transform judgement into empathy and connection.

Introducing the JUDGE method

To help navigate and transform this habit of judgement, I have created a simple yet powerful tool: the JUDGE Method. This easy-to-remember acronym stands for Jot it down, Understand the Context, Determine Alternative Perspectives, Generate Empathy, and Embrace and Release.

The JUDGE Method is a practical, step-by-step approach designed to help you catch, analyse, and shift judgemental thoughts. By following these steps, it will help you gradually move from a mindset of criticism to one of understanding and empathy. Whether you're dealing with self-judgement or feelings towards others, the JUDGE Method offers a structured and flexible framework to help transform how you perceive and interact with the world.

Here is how you can implement JUDGE in everyday situations to help you lead a Self-Led Life®.

J: Jot down the judgement

When you notice a judgement of yourself or another person, as soon as you catch yourself, jot it down on your phone, notepad, or whatever works for you. It helps to see it visually, it's impactful!

U: Understand the context

Reflect on the context or situation that led to this judgement to help give you a broader perspective and understand the circumstances that may have influenced the behaviour or thought, either yours or someone else's.

D: Determine alternative perspectives

Consider different angles or perspectives that could explain the situation or behaviour to open your mind to other possibilities and reasons, moving away from a single, judgemental viewpoint.

G: Generate empathy

Replace your initial judgement with a statement of empathy, or understanding, to practise empathy and shift your attitude from criticism to compassion.

E: Embrace and release

Acknowledge the effort you've made in transforming your judgement and mentally let go of it to help strengthen positive changes in your thought process and to consciously release the judgemental attitude.

This journey from judgement to acceptance and understanding is ongoing. It's not about perfection; it's about progress. Each step you take towards accepting and understanding yourself and others is a step towards a more peaceful and fulfilling life. Clocking any judgements you have is another part of the Therapeutic relationship, taking this learning and using it in everyday life, I think we could all benefit from being more aware of the judgements we experience.

Summary

- We all judge ourselves and others.
- Judgement affects the ability to build relationships.
- Judgement is often an automatic response based on personal beliefs.
- With self-awareness, we can understand the root causes and make changes.

Self-Led Life® inspired actions

- Use the JUDGE Method.
- Writing down judgements can be very powerful when you see them; it will help you to explore.
- Use judgements as a way to strengthen your skills in empathy.

15

Using fierce self-compassion on the journey to YOU

This was another amazing insight for me I discovered as part of my research on authenticity. The power is being able to access my fierce but loving 'Mama Bear' to practise self-compassion. It's a way of standing up for yourself whilst being kind at the same time, defending your well-being and being your self-led hero. Inspired by Dr Kristin Neff.

What is fierce self-compassion? Fierce self-compassion at its core is about embodying the fierce, protective energy of a mother bear defending her cubs. This translates to strongly protecting your own well-being and mental health. It's about empowering yourself to stand up against internal and external negative forces much like how a Mama Bear has the instinct to defend against threats to her young.

Assertiveness and strength. It encourages assertiveness. It's about recognising when you are being too hard yourself or when others are overstepping your boundaries. Assertiveness in this context means speaking up for yourself saying no when needed and not being passive in the face of self-criticism or external judgement.

Active love and care. The Mama Bear approach is a form of active love. It is not passive or merely about feeling compassion internally it's about putting that compassion into action. This might mean taking steps to change harmful habits, setting boundaries to protect your emotional health or actively working towards your personal goals.

Negative self-talk. A big part of this approach is combating negative self-talk. The Mama Bear doesn't tolerate harmful, self-critical thoughts. Instead, she confronts these thoughts with fierce love and counteracts them with affirming positive self-talk.

Self-empowerment. Fierce self-compassion is intrinsically linked to self-leadership. It is about taking charge of your well-being, not waiting for external validation or permission. It involves making choices that prioritise your needs and support your growth.

Balance of Yin and Yang. Whilst the Mama Bear approach emphasises the more assertive aspects of self-compassion, it's balanced by the gentler, more nurturing aspects (the Yin). This balance ensures a holistic approach to self-care, where you learn to be both gentle and fierce in your self-compassion practice.

Be your biggest fan. Finally, the Mama Bear approach is about advocacy - being your advocate in situations where your interests, values, or well-being are at stake. It is about having the courage to stand up for what you need and deserve, both from yourself and others. In essence, the Mama Bear approach to self-compassion is about harnessing the power of a powerful blend of love, strength and protectiveness towards yourself. It is a dynamic and active way of practising self-care that advocates for a strong stance against anything that compromises your mental and emotional health.

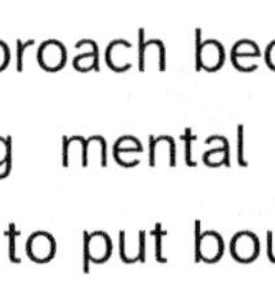

I chose to use this approach because it involves taking action and prioritising mental well-being, this really spoke to me. I wanted to put boundaries in place that I knew would be a challenge, I found it helpful having Mama Bear around protecting me for me. It was a more direct way of leading myself away from people pleasing,

I love how this approach appreciates the protective part, Mama Bear aligns with the other learning and helps you to take an assertive action. It works for me as it's not just about accepting myself it's about truly standing up for myself and saying 'I matter, my feelings matter, and I'm not settling for less', Being your advocate in situations where your interests, values or well-being are at stake. It is about having the courage to stand up for what you need and deserve, both from yourself and others.

Summary

- We can be fierce and friendly when we practise self-compassion.
- A way of remaining compassionate while being assertive.
- Mama Bear prioritises your mental health.

Self-Led Life® inspired actions

- Be your advocate and protect your mental health
- Take action

These two insight exercises will help you access your very own Mama Bear.

1. Visualisation and Reflection

Find a comfortable, quiet space where you can be reflective without interruptions.

Close your eyes, take several deep breaths, and bring to mind a situation where you felt a need to protect yourself or stand up for your well-being.

In your mind, give shape to your protective instinct. Imagine it as a 'Mama Bear.' What qualities does she have? Strength, warmth, courage, assertiveness?

Open your eyes and write down all the attributes of your 'Mama Bear' that came to mind. Don't overthink it; let the words flow naturally.

Recall and Relate

Think of three instances in your life when you successfully stood up for yourself or set a necessary boundary. What qualities did you show?

Write down these instances and the qualities you displayed during these times.

Connect and Personalise

Look at the traits you've written down. Circle the ones that appear both in your visualisation and in your real-life examples.

From the circled attributes, choose the top three that resonate most with you — these are the core qualities of your 'Mama Bear.'

Affirmation and Application

Create a personal affirmation that includes these three attributes. For example, "With the strength, courage, and warmth of my inner Mama Bear, I protect my peace and stand up for my needs."

Reflect on how you can apply these qualities in daily life to advocate for yourself and others. Write one actionable step for each attribute.

2. Practice Mama Bear responses to help with boundaries

Consider areas in your life where your boundaries are not respected, and you feel the need to advocate for yourself.

Write down one action you can take to enforce a boundary, inspired by your 'Mama Bear' energy. This could be as simple as saying “no” to an additional commitment or standing up for yourself in a relationship.

Compassionate Action

Identify one thing you have been harshly criticizing yourself for.

Write a letter to yourself from the perspective of the 'Mama Bear'—full of understanding, protection, and encouragement.

Read this letter back to yourself whenever you need a reminder of your inner strength and compassion.

16
Letting Go of the Need for Approval

In the journey towards authenticity, the only approval that truly matters is your own.

As you walk the path to discovering your true self, one of the biggest hurdles you might face is the deep-rooted need for approval from others. It is a natural desire, stemming from your innate social instincts. However, when this need overshadows your internal locus of control - your belief in your ability to control your own life - it can steer you away from your authentic path.

Impact

The continuous search for external validation can lead you into a trap. It's like handing over the compass of your life to someone else, letting their opinions and judgements dictate your direction. This dependence on external validation can cloud your self-perception and delay your personal growth.

Shifting your locus of control inward

Remember the concept of locus of control you've explored earlier? Recognise that your thoughts, actions, and feelings are under your control, not someone else's. Your internal locus of control is empowering – it's about taking the lead in your life and guiding yourself according to your values and beliefs, not the expectations of others.

Strategies for letting go of approval-seeking

1. **Recognise your worth**: Understand that your worth comes from inside you and not determined by others' opinions.
2. **Mindfulness and self-awareness**: Practise mindfulness to become more aware of moments when you seek external validation.
3. **Set boundaries**: Learn to set healthy boundaries with others. It is okay to say no and to prioritise your needs and feelings, ask Mama Bear, she will help you!

4. **Reflect on your values**: Revisit your core values. Are your actions aligned with these, or are they more aligned with pleasing others? Remember to use your values as a guide to direct your decisions.
5. **Celebrate Your Individuality**: Embrace and celebrate what makes you unique. Your individuality is your strength, not something that needs approval from others.

Overcoming the fear of disapproval

1. **Get curious about your fears**: When you fear disapproval, ask yourself, "What's really going on here? What belief is this attached to **that's not mine!"**
2. **Seek Constructive Feedback**: Instead of seeking approval, seek constructive feedback that aids your growth. There's a difference between wanting to be liked and wanting to grow.
3. **Self-compassion**: Be kind to yourself during this process. Letting go of the need for approval is challenging but incredibly rewarding.

Releasing the need for external approval and embracing your internal locus of control is a powerful and effective step towards authenticity. It is about trusting yourself and honouring your journey, knowing that the most important approval comes from within. As you continue this path, work on improving your independence and feel the freedom that comes with being the true author of your life story.

Summary

- It is natural to seek approval from others.
- Awareness will help you to shift your locus internally in these moments.
- Use your values as a benchmark to guide you.

Self-Led Life® inspired actions

- Recognise the importance of the position of your locus.
- Use this to recognise the importance of having a clear understanding of values at all times to help guide you.

17
ACT & RFT to manage self-doubt and negative thinking

I want to briefly introduce you to an alternative way of dealing with self-doubt and negative thoughts. While it's common practice to question and reframe thoughts, there is also another approach which I also use. ACT Therapy was developed by Steven C. Hayes. I struggled to stop some of the negative thoughts I was having especially regarding my health anxiety. This approach works well for me as it allows me to live alongside my negative thoughts instead of getting rid of them, they are there but I am not controlled by them. Below is a summary, more information about ACT is available on my website.

Relational Frame Theory (RFT)

RFT is a theory of language and cognition. It suggests

that the human ability to understand and create language is based on learning to relate things in different ways. For instance, we learn that one thing is similar to another, through connections, called "relational frames." We can compare things (like "bigger," or "smaller"), see how they're the same or different, and even think about time (like "yesterday" or "tomorrow"). This helps us understand complex ideas and solve problems. But sometimes, our superpower gets us tangled up. With RFT, psychologists try to understand how we link ideas, how language influences our behaviour, and why we think and feel the way we do.

Acceptance and Commitment Therapy (ACT)

ACT is dedicated to enhancing people's lives, Instead of solely battling symptoms, which can diminish life satisfaction, ACT focuses on elevating life quality, regardless of symptom fluctuation. Despite uncontrollable factors, there are always opportunities to improve our lives. ACT helps people understand that they are not defined by their condition or illness. It advocates for the possibility of leading a meaningful and fulfilling life, aligned with personal values, even amid mental illness. This understanding can be transformative.

Self-doubt and ACT

Acceptance and Commitment Therapy (ACT) is particularly useful for dealing with self-doubt. It helps you to respond mindfully to harsh or critical thoughts.

Self-doubt includes **thoughts and feelings** such as wondering whether you can succeed at important activities, having thoughts that focus on the bad things that might occur and feeling unsure about your abilities. As a result of all that feeling, you can feel like a failure if you have avoided doing the things you want to because self-doubt has got in the way of you achieving success. A small degree of self-doubt can however be helpful to you as it can lead you to analyse and inspect your behaviour and thought patterns. If self-doubt becomes unbearable, affecting your daily functioning, or affects your performance at work or school then a therapist or other mental health professional may be able to offer support and guidance.

Self-esteem

One of the aspects of self-doubt is self-esteem in particular low self-esteem as it relates to issues, such as negative repetitive thinking, self-criticism low self-worth, mistrust towards others, self-blame, or feeling unlike you or unfairly treated. This thinking can lead to tension or anxiety adding to psychological and even physical issues. When you hear self-doubt what comes to your mind, do you ever self-doubt? Do you think confident people ever doubt themselves? We all experience self-doubt including confident and successful people, everybody ponders whether they did the right thing, or questioned something, it's just the fact that making a decision comes quicker to some than to others and this can make people appear more confident. Self-doubt is a normal occurrence which tends to get worse if you don't pay attention to it and don't take action to raise your self-esteem.

Self-doubting behaviours

Other behaviours that tend to stem from having self-doubt can include seeking other people's advice and seeking constant validity that you have made the right decision. Often this can lead to an anxious type of self-doubt especially if you are used to having anxiety in the first place, it would be fair to say that anxiety and self-doubt go hand-in-hand, but self-doubt doesn't mean that you have anxiety. Whereas anxious people may experience more self-doubts than people without anxiety and people without anxiety can experience self-doubt as a normal occurrence. Another problem with self-doubting is that high levels of self-doubt can lead to reduced effort in making decisions, planning productivity, in general performance and coping with challenges. Self-doubt is a normal response to situations where the person experiences failure and lack of success but what a person does and how they cope with the issue is what leads to either increased self-doubt or successful performance afterwards.

Seeking approval

Over time self-doubt can lead to a persistent need for assurance leaving you feeling anxious unless others are providing it to you. It can leave people paralysed when making decisions; fearing they made the wrong choice or you might get stuck on everything from which career to pursue to which bed sheet to purchase. The problem with self-doubt is that it prevents you from expressing your true self as you might compromise your authentic voice while seeking confirmation from others. Low self-esteem and self-criticism can be overcome with the practice of tools such as accepting your thoughts and feelings, choosing a value direction and taking action mindfully. Self-doubt and confidence levels do go hand-in-hand but ACT teaches the thoughts that result from self-doubt are just thoughts and are not something that you cannot change, with ACT you learn to observe the thoughts like either the clouds in the sky or something else that comes and goes.

Empowerment and Self-Compassion:

ACT helps you create a sense of empowerment and self-compassion, encouraging individuals to treat themselves kindly and recognise their ability to make positive changes, despite the presence of self-doubt. In summary, ACT's holistic approach, which includes accepting thoughts, focusing on actionable values, and developing psychological flexibility, makes it a powerful tool for managing self-doubt and fostering a more positive and action-oriented mindset.

Summary

- ACT is part of the Relational Frame Theory.
- **Focuses on both thoughts and feelings.**
- Long-Term Benefits - one of the strengths of ACT is its focus on long-term change. Studies have shown that the benefits of ACT, such as increased psychological flexibility and improved mental health, can be sustained over time.

Self-Led Life® inspired actions

- Use mindfulness to heighten self-awareness, making it easier to understand your true feelings and reactions to various situations.
- Set goals and engage in behaviours that are in harmony with your values, even in the face of difficulties or challenges.

Here are some Insights to help learn more about Acceptance and Commitment Therapy (ACT) techniques to manage self-doubt:

Accept your thoughts: Understand that it's natural to experience self-doubt. Instead of fighting these thoughts, acknowledge and accept them as part of your inner experience. Remember, these thoughts don't define your capabilities or worth.

Practise mindfulness: Engage in mindfulness practices. This could mean taking a few minutes each day to sit quietly and observe your thoughts and feelings without judgement. Mindfulness helps you become more aware of the present moment and less entangled in the web of self-doubt.

Identify your values: Reflect on what truly matters to you. What are your core values? Identifying these can guide your actions and decisions, leading you toward a life that feels more meaningful and fulfilling, even when self-doubt arises.

Take committed action: Set small, achievable goals that align with your values. Taking action, despite the presence of self-doubt, reinforces your ability to move forward and builds confidence in your capacity to handle challenges.

Use cognitive diffusion Techniques: Practise techniques that help you see thoughts as just thoughts, not absolute truths. For example, when you notice self-doubt, you might mentally say, "I'm having the thought that I am not good enough," instead of "I am not good enough." This subtle shift can reduce the impact of negative thoughts.

Develop psychological flexibility: Support the ability to adapt to various situations with openness and awareness. When self-doubt surfaces, recognise it, and then consciously choose how you'll respond in a way that aligns with your values.

Be kind to yourself: Treat yourself with the same kindness and compassion you would offer a good friend. Self-compassion is a powerful antidote to self-doubt. Remember, everyone experiences doubts and fears; you're not alone in this.

Reframe

Psychologists recommend you can also manage self-doubts by re-framing your thoughts by recognising your doubt as something else, or you could try to distinguish between realistic and unrealistic self-doubt. You can examine how rational your thoughts are by asking yourself questions, whether you've done something similar in the past and whether your self-doubts are real. Are they based on something valid, unquestionable or part of your fearful self? Instead, you could also manage your doubts by reducing your standards of how well you're doing something or are you trying be a perfectionist? Try to remember everybody is different. You can introduce new thinking, 'I do as best as I can but it's ok whatever the outcome is, I have no reason to worry, I'll enjoy the process and learn something new'. This thinking can help lower self-doubt. Some of us tend to seek validation and reassurance from others and at times realise we know the information ourselves but we just cannot stop ourselves from seeking advice. ACT encourages you to trust yourself, whatever you decide is good enough. When you seek others' advice over your own you send the message internally that you are not good enough, you can learn to trust yourself by committing to making a decision on your own. Part of living a Self-Led Life® is building confidence in yourself that only you know what is truly best for you.

ACT uses great metaphors to help us understand and accept, here are my favourites.

Passengers on the bus

Imagine being the driver of your life's bus. You're in charge of the speed and direction, navigating a road that's important to you—a road where overcoming challenges, big or small, is part of the journey.

This bus carries a mix of passengers: your thoughts, feelings, emotions, sensations, and memories. Some cheer you on, while others, like the loud inner critic, demand attention and critique you. They can be distracting, often leading you to try different tactics to quiet them.

Compliance: You might think doing what these demanding passengers say will keep the peace. However, this usually results in veering off your desired path.

Confrontation: Arguing with these passengers can be draining and often doesn't lead to long-term silence or peace.

Resistance: You may try to power through by ignoring them, which can make steering your life's bus even harder.

Acceptance: It's about recognising that these passengers, including your pain, are part of your journey right now. Acceptance isn't surrendering; it's a strategic acknowledgement that lets you refocus on driving towards a meaningful life.

Diffusion and Mindfulness: Realise that thoughts are just thoughts, not facts. With mindfulness, you observe your thoughts and feelings without getting wrapped up in them, enabling you to address pain more effectively.

Values and commitment: Identify what truly matters to you and commit to actions that align with these values. Pain might be on the bus, but it doesn't have to control where it goes. By committing to value-driven actions, it helps you to lead a fulfilling life despite the pain.

** There are some great clips on YouTube search ACT passengers on the bus **

Keep your distance!

Another technique to create some distance between your mind and thoughts is where you imagine little soldiers coming out of your ears and walking away into the distance in front of your nose holding banners with the thoughts written in them. Each new thought goes on a sign in this never-ending parade of tiny soldiers. The signs carry words, images, and even sounds and voices.

The point is that you imagine watching your mind's activities from a distance as the thought parade goes by. Or another way is, let your thoughts float by like leaves flowing in a stream, as clouds in the sky, or as credits on a movie screen.

These strategies aren't quick fixes—they require practice. But with time, they can help build resilience, allow you to live meaningfully, and regain a sense of control. Remember, while you can't always choose your passengers, you do have the power to steer your bus towards your desired destination.

This information is not a substitute for therapy, it is for the purpose of providing tools that you may find useful as part of self-development, please seek the help of a professional therapist who specialises in ACT Therapy or visit gericarey.com

18
Why journaling works

Like looking in the mirror, some of you won't like the idea of writing and find it uncomfortable, and that's ok. Lots of people tell me that they wouldn't know where to start, or they fancy the idea and don't get around to it. I started by writing a family diary and it went from there, there have been times I've written things, got them off my chest and then thrown them in the bin! It is about finding the small moments to connect with your inside world. The goal of journaling is not to create a literary masterpiece but to provide a space for honest and personal reflection. Journaling can be more than just a record of your days, It allows you to unravel the layers of your experiences, bringing to light the values that shape and define you.

Clear your mind: Writing helps in organising and getting clear about your thoughts. As you put pen to paper, you transform intangible feelings and ideas into concrete words, making it easier to understand and analyse them.

Let it go: Journaling provides a safe outlet for expressing emotions. It can be particularly therapeutic in processing complex or overwhelming feelings, helping you to identify and understand the emotions tied to your experiences.

Find your themes and patterns: Regular journaling allows you to spot patterns in your thoughts and behaviours over time or you may even find your owl! You might start to notice recurring themes or issues that are important to you, which can point towards your underlying values.

Problem-Solving: Writing about challenges or dilemmas can often lead to new perspectives and solutions. It encourages you to approach problems from different angles, deepening your understanding of what truly matters in these situations.

Fancy something different?

If just journaling isn't for you why not collect data? Visit my website gericarey.com to learn more about how to do your own mini self-inquiry research.

- As you go about your day, and take photos, collect artefacts that stand out to you such as a rock, pebble, shell etc, things that grab your attention.
- Capture your glimmers, take a voice note or scrapbook and note what makes you feel excited that day. This could be a song you haven't heard for ages, a conversation with someone, or anything that gets you revved up a little.
- Capture your dimmers, and take note of anything that's brought the mood down, conversations, feelings etc.
- Leave it to incubate! Put the data to one side and leave it for at least a week while you go about your business.
- Return to it and put it all together, can you spot any themes? Did you spot any patterns in your glimmers and dimmers, did they connect, leading you to a bigger story? For example, did they most appear around a certain person or hobby or place? This gives you a great idea of what to do more and less of!

Everyone deserves to unlock their potential, and self-research techniques are the key! Discovering more about yourself isn't just enlightening—it's revolutionary. Knowing yourself deeply is the first step to leading a powerful, Self-Led Life®.

19
Self-regulation SUPER POWER

Think of it like the inner thermostat for your emotions and reactions. It is what helps you keep cool when you're about to snap at someone or when you're tempted by that extra slice of cake. Self-regulation is all about managing your impulses and emotions in a way that fits with your long-term goals. It is like having a smart inner voice that says, “Hold up, let's think this through” before you make a move. And the best part? It is a skill you can get better at with practice.

What is “self-regulation” all about? It is your superpower for staying in charge of your feelings and actions. Imagine you're driving a car. Self-regulation is like having a good grip on the steering wheel, regardless if the road is smooth or full of potholes. Whether it's passing a test, getting a new job, or not losing your temper in traffic. How you manage your inner world makes all the difference. It keeps your stress in check and helps you manage setbacks from tough times. There is a bit of science behind this, your prefrontal cortex, right behind your forehead, is the command centre for self-regulation. It is the logic of making sure you think things through instead of just reacting automatically. It is all about strengthening that brain muscle. And guess what? Just like any skill, you can get better at it with a bit of practice.

Awareness

The first crucial aspect of self-regulation is awareness. This is about being mindful of your actions and emotions. Imagine having an inner observer that helps you notice when you're procrastinating or becoming overly emotional. Awareness is like a real-time self-monitoring tool, providing insights into your behaviours and feelings.

Standards - your personal rulebook

Consider the idea of personal standards. These are the values, rules and goals you set for yourself based on what matters to you. It could be maintaining honesty, achieving fitness goals, or managing stress effectively. These standards are benchmarks that guide your behaviour and decisions. They are the 'personal bests' you aim to achieve and live by every day.

Mindfulness techniques to sharpen self-awareness

Mindfulness is a powerful tool for self-regulation. It involves paying attention to the present moment without judgement. Practising mindfulness can cultivate a deeper understanding of your thoughts, feelings, and actions.

Managing your emotional landscape

Handling emotions healthily is a key part of self-regulation. It is about recognising, understanding, and responding to your emotions in a way that is beneficial for you and those around you.

Reflection instead of reaction

When a strong emotion hits, take a moment to pause. Reflect on why you're feeling this way. This pause can prevent knee-jerk reactions and help you respond more thoughtfully.

Constructive expression

Find healthy ways to express your emotions. This could be through talking to someone you trust, writing in a journal, or engaging in a creative activity like painting or listening to music.

Seeking support

Remember, it's okay to ask for help. Talking to friends, family, or a professional can provide you with different perspectives and coping mechanisms.

Self-regulation helps you achieve goals

Long-term vision: Self-regulation helps maintain focus on long-term goals, steering you through distractions and short-term gains.

Emotional management: It involves understanding and managing your emotions effectively, ensuring they don't derail you from your path.

Impulse control: This aspect of self-regulation is crucial in resisting temptations that don't align with your goals.

Implementing self-regulation in relationships

- Practise self-regulation in your interactions. Respond thoughtfully, even in emotionally charged situations.
- Use self-regulation to foster empathy. Recognise and respect the feelings of others, even when they differ from yours.
- Understand that self-regulation is a skill that has its limits. Fatigue, stress, and external pressures can impact your ability to self-regulate.
- Be kind to yourself when you face difficulties in regulating your responses. Self-compassion is a key component of emotional resilience.

Self-regulation is an active and ongoing practice. It is a key component of emotional intelligence and a crucial factor in achieving personal fulfilment and authenticity.

As you develop and refine your self-regulation skills,

you'll find that it not only helps you realise your personal goals but also enriches your relationships and enhances your overall quality of life.

Summary

- Your inner thermostat for your emotions and reactions
- It helps you to recognise and understand emotions
- Develops mindfulness
- Helps build relationships
- Helps with resilience

Self-Led Life® inspired actions

- Consistently practise self-awareness to understand emotional triggers and patterns.
- Set clear, achievable goals and prioritise tasks effectively.
- Actively work on maintaining emotional balance.
- Flexible and open to change.
- Listen actively and communicate with empathy.

20

Discovering YOUR Purpose: Guided by Positive Psychology Insights

Martin Seligman introduced positive psychology in 1998, a new branch of psychology which focussed on the study of positive emotions, character strengths, and building a flourishing life. Until then, psychology had generally focused on the problems people faced, what was wrong in their lives, and how it contributed to their depression, anxiety, and lack of mental well-being.

Seligman's theory suggests we humans have **five** basic psychological needs:

- To feel positive emotion.
- Engage in activities that give life meaning and purpose.
- Have positive relationships with others.
- Find meaning and fulfilment in what we do.
- Savour achievements and accomplishments.

Striving to achieve them all together leads to the development of personal well-being and the opportunity to flourish. Seligman also suggests that individuals have the capacity to develop and strengthen their character strengths, such as grit, resilience, and gratitude, which can further help to enhance their well-being and increase happiness. (Seligman, 2011).

PERMA – A positive psychology model

The PERMA model is Seligman's framework for understanding and measuring well-being.

It is evidence-based and a valuable and powerful tool for therapy and our personal and working lives. The PERMA model proposes we can break down well-being into five key elements: Positive emotions, Engagement, Relationships, Meaning, and Accomplishment.

Positive emotion: Positive emotions refer to the experience of positive feelings and emotions, such as satisfaction, awe, joy, and contentment.

Engagement: When you engage deeply with your activities, you often encounter what Seligman calls 'flow' - those moments where time seems to stand still. There is a clue to finding activities that align with your purpose.

Relationships: Strong positive relationships can support and shape your understanding of your purpose. They offer different perspectives and can be a source of inspiration and encouragement.

Meaning: According to Seligman meaning comes from serving something beyond us. Finding your purpose involves identifying how you can contribute to the greater good, in ways that resonate with your personal values and strengths.

Accomplishment: Setting and achieving goals related to your purpose brings a sense of accomplishment. This is not about external markers of success but about fulfilling your potential and making a meaningful impact.

Remember to use the book companion and to head to gericarey.com for more ways that positive psychology can help you on your way to discover your true self.

These insights will provide strategies to help you to start using PERMA as a way of supporting your growth.

The power of flow

Imagine diving into an activity that captures your whole being, an experience so engaging that it feels like a dance between you and the task at hand. This is the realm of flow, a concept that Mihaly Csikszentmihalyi, a renowned psychologist brought into the spotlight.

As you start the journey to discover and embrace your true self, the concept of flow holds the clues. It's not just about finding the moments of enjoyment; it's about aligning your actions with your deepest passions, values, and abilities. Think of flow as your guide to self-actualisation. In these moments of deep absorption, you're not only performing at your best, you're also experiencing a version of yourself that is often hidden in the bustle of everyday life. The state of flow isn't for just artists, athletes or musicians. It is accessible to everybody, in any activity that resonates with their true self. Whether you find it in writing, gardening, coding, teaching or even in the simplicity of a mindful walk, flow is there waiting to be discovered.

Deep Dive: In flow your laser focus is sharp. It is like the world around you fades away leaving only you. The task is a complete concentration that is not forced and a natural alignment of your attention with the activity. Imagine reading a book and being so engrossed that you don't hear the clock tick and that's the essence of this deep focus, effortless yet all-consuming.

Empowering mastery: This isn't about controlling the outcome, it is about feeling in control of your actions and decisions in the moment. There is a sense of mastery that comes with flow, where you feel capable and competent.

Freedom from self: In flow, self-consciousness dissolves. You're not thinking about how you look, how you're perceived, or even your usual self-doubts. It is a liberating escape from the inner critic. This loss of self-consciousness allows you to express yourself fully, without the filter of self-judgement. It is in these moments that you trust your abilities will shine through.

Joy in the journey: What drives you in flow is not external rewards but the pleasure of the activity itself. It is about doing something for the sheer joy of it. This deep-rooted motivation is what makes flow so rewarding and sustainable.

Achieving flow in your life

Flow is not just a state of mind, it's a lifestyle, a way to live in harmony with your true self and these insights will give you practical strategies to help you step into flow regularly.

Identifying activities that light you up

Reflect on activities that make you lose track of time, that both challenge and fulfil you. These could be hobbies, work related tasks, or even every day chores done in a certain way. Remember flow can be found in the most unexpected places.

Align with your values

Aligning activities with your core values and strengths is crucial for finding flow, setting clear goals.

Goal setting techniques

Set goals that are both challenging and achievable, aligning with your personal growth strategy.

Seek challenges

Find the right level of challenge, understand how to gauge the right level of challenge to enter flow without feeling overwhelmed.

Minimise distractions

Create the right environment to encourage flow whether at home, work, or in public spaces; this includes managing physical and digital distractions.

Focus on the process not the outcome

Focus on the present moment and the process of your activity, rather than being solely outcome driven. This approach is key to achieving flow.

Steps to uncover your true values through peak experiences

Have you ever had any moments in your life when you have felt at your absolute best - utterly fulfilled, genuinely happy, or incredibly proud. These aren't just fleeting moments of joy, they're experiences that leave a lasting impact and provide deep insights into your core values. Reflecting on these experiences is like looking through a window into your soul, revealing what truly matters to you on the deepest level.

Identifying your peak moments

Can you remember the times in your life when you have felt exceptionally content, accomplished, or connected. These could be big life events, like career achievement, or quieter moments like a meaningful conversation with a close friend. It is helpful to look across the different areas of your life; at personal achievements, relationships, professional successes, recreational activities, and even moments of solitude.

For each peak experience delve into the details of what were you doing. Who were you with? Where were you? What was happening around you? Try to recall how you felt in that moment. Were you exhilarated, at peace or deeply satisfied? What about that experience evokes these feelings?

Understand the power

Reflect on why each experience stands out; was it the sense of accomplishment, the feeling of being connected to others, the thrill of overcoming a challenge, or the joy of learning something new? Sometimes the significance of a peak experience isn't immediately apparent. Take your time to explore the underlying reasons why these moments were so impactful.

Identifying themes

Look for patterns or themes that emerge across your different peak experiences. For example, if many of your peak moments involve helping others, a core value might be compassionate service. If you feel most alive while tackling challenges, perhaps personal growth or resilience are significant values for you.

Connecting experiences to values

Use these themes to identify your core values. These are values that guide you through the principles of your life, understanding them is useful for making decisions that lead to more fulfilling authentic experiences. Write down these values and consider how they've shaped your choices and life path so far. This reflection can provide profound insights into your true self and guide you into setting future goals.

Journaling

Write about your previous experiences in detail in a journal describing the feelings, the people involved, the setting, and why each experience was meaningful. This experience can help solidify your understanding of your values.

Visual representation

You could also create a visual representation of your peak experiences such as a photo collage or a mind map. This can be a powerful way to connect emotionally with these moments and what they reveal about your news.

Sharing with others

Sometimes, discussing your peak experiences with a trusted friend or family member can offer new perspectives and insights. These moments can deepen your understanding and affirmation of your core values.

(R) Cultivate positive relationships

Surround yourself with people who inspire and challenge you. Engage in conversations about life's big questions and listen to other perspectives on purpose and fulfilment. On the road to self-discovery every interaction is a step for growth - some comfort, some challenge, but all contribute to your journey. Life is too short.

Unsupportive relationships

Not all people will be supportive, some may be rooted in their own fears and insecurities - managing unsupportive relationships is a complex yet important part of your path to self. It teaches you to approach yourself and others with empathy understanding and resilience. As you move forward use your new skills such as self-compassion and the deeper understanding of other peoples' perspectives. Unsupportive relationships often reflect the challenges and insecurities of the other person. Recognising this can help you approach these situations with empathy. It is not uncommon for people to react negatively to change, especially if it alters the dynamic of your relationship that they are comfortable with.

Strategies for handling unsupportive relationships

As we have been learning all along we are all so different and our experiences of unsupportive relationships will never be the same. If a person close to you is preventing you from making a change you would like to make, or if you are facing any cultural barriers please be self-led and seek the help and support of a professional therapist or organisation that's specific to your situation.

Reflect on reactions

Understand that other people's reactions to your growth can stem from their fear of change or loss. It is natural for people to resist changes that disrupt their sense of normality. It is tempting to react if someone is not being supportive; remind yourself it's what you think that matters.

Cultivate self-compassion

Be kind to yourself when facing resistance. Remember your journey is about your growth and well-being and it's ok to prioritise these.

Effective communication

Engage in open conversations. Express how those supportive conversations are valuable to you and how their supportiveness affects you.

Set healthy boundaries

While empathy is important, setting boundaries is crucial for your well-being. Gently, but firmly, establish what behaviours you can and can't accept.

Focus on your journey

Keep your focus on your goals and personal growth. Surround yourself with civility and those who genuinely support your journey.

Navigate emotional reactions to change

Change can be intimidating, not just for you but also for those around you. Some may fear losing the relationship they have with you or feel insecure about their place in your changing life.

Balancing empathy and personal growth

Striving to balance empathy for others with your need for personal growth is a delicate dance between understanding their perspective and not compromising on your journey.

Transitioning towards supportive relationships

As you learn to manage unsupportive relationships, the importance of nurturing supportive relationships becomes clear. This will help you to build your growth circle - people who understand, celebrate and contribute to your growth.

Nurturing your growth circle

Your growth circle is an essential part of your very ecosystem. It is a community that you cultivate, one that nurtures your personal development and enriches your journey. In this circle, every relationship is an opportunity to learn, grow, and move closer to the person you aspire to be. Creating a growth circle that is designed and nurtured by you will help you in so many ways. The people in our lives are like mirrors and windows into our potential so choose those who reflect the best and inspire you to look beyond. This isn't just about you choosing the friends that can fit on one hand, it's more than that. Nor is it about having a full circle. It is about making sure that you are getting the right level of support from people.

Define your growth circle

There is a handy section in your book companion and a printable PDF. To help bring this to life visit gericarey.com

When I first did this exercise some time ago, I found it hard. My circle is now small and safe, it has taken time and a lot of courage to build, however, it's now a part of the very foundation that supports my growth. Who are the people who encourage you to push your boundaries, share in your successes, and provide comfort and guidance during challenging times? If you can't think of anyone, was there anyone in your past?

Recruit your circle members

Reflect on past interactions and think about times when you have felt particularly inspired, supported or challenged in a positive way.

- Who was involved?
- What role did they play?
- What qualities do they have? Is it their ability to listen, their wisdom, or perhaps their honesty?
- What values do they have?
- What was/is special about your relationship?
- How do you complement their growth?
- How do they complement your growth?
- Is it their positivity?
- How can you also contribute to their growth?

Set the standards for new members

Use your new insights as a benchmark for future members.

Building and strengthening your growth circle

Regular check-ins: Establish regular communication with your circle. Find out what communication works for you and them, meetups, phone calls, voice notes etc. My friends and I can't always find the time at the moment to call so instead we voice note wherever we can. It is a great way to stay in touch and to give and receive support when you can't be tied to the end of the phone or sit and text. Another friend loves a call at a set time each week as I drive to work and another friend who lives down South meets me in the middle of the country every three to four months for a face-to-face catch-up. Sounds straightforward but sometimes I think we assume people might want to be contacted and it's always worth a simple check-in. I know some of my friends would not appreciate my podcast length voice notes and others look forward to them.

Shared growth activities: Engage in activities that promote your mutual growth, do you have anything in common? Or can they help you learn a new skill? Can you go for a cold-water dip or a spa, maybe a walk, shopping, a run, cycle or art class? If you spot an activity a friend would like, let them know.

Feedback and reflection: Encourage an environment where open and constructive feedback is welcomed regularly to reflect on what you learn from each other. This is the key to this relationship being open to the other person's view and making sure you both feel you can be honest. Draw on therapy insights, practise empathy, promote positive self-regard and be aware of your congruence.

Do not stop there: Your growth circle should evolve as you do. Some relationships may grow stronger while others might fade away and that's ok, it's a natural part of growth and development. Try not to take things personally. You will often find if you have built the relationship on the above strong foundations, you may well sense if the person is drifting away. It is often the case if our direction changes, so does our circle. But with the above foundations you will appreciate their position and they will appreciate yours and no doubt will be able to reassess the communication and connection that works for both of you.

Disagreements and conflicts can still arise even in the most positive relationships. Approach these with an open mind and aim for resolution and understanding. Not every argument has to end with somebody winning or choosing to part ways. It is important to set healthy boundaries in all relationships. Understand and communicate your limits clearly. Sometimes reaching out and maintaining connections can be daunting especially if you're introverted so start with small steps and gradually expand your comfort zone.

(M) Meaning

Seek meaning beyond yourself, engage in volunteer work, community service or other activities that contribute to something larger than your personal gains and notice how these experiences make you feel.

Finding time

Finding your meaning or purpose is magical as it is what keeps you connected to yourself, having more than material things. What is my purpose is one of the most common questions we ask ourselves, what is the meaning of life? In between all of the hustle and bustle of everyday life, it can be hard to find a purpose or even think that there is anything different for you to do.

Can money help me?

I thought I would get to my purpose of finding happiness through financial success, but as we have learned it doesn't always make you fulfilled. Research indicates that achieving such "extrinsic" goals is not necessarily associated with greater happiness. I think that money can affect happiness to a certain extent, I think money can help you to lean into what lights you up and try new experiences. It is about balance and awareness, so for example, if you work long hours to keep the house and mortgage payments and you're not getting the time to look or experience glimmers then you may find yourself feeling stuck. If you are struggling and want to explore resilience this is the perfect time to recommend Man's Search for Meaning by Viktor E Frankl. He shows that even in the most horrific circumstances life can be given meaning through how we choose to respond to those circumstances and the attitude we take towards unavoidable suffering. He explores the idea that finding purpose and meaning in life is key to personal resilience and psychological well-being. He emphasises the importance of hope, choice, and finding significance in life challenges.

(A) Accomplishment or achievement

A refers to the pursuit of success, mastery, or achievement for its own sake. It is about setting goals, working towards them and feeling a sense of satisfaction and fulfilment upon achieving them. Accomplishment is important in the model because it encourages you to be self-led; it can be a source of deep-rooted motivation. It is not just about external things but also about personal growth and the feeling of having achieved something significant regardless of recognition or reward from others.

Discovering true north, your compass values

Your values are the core beliefs and principles that govern your every decision and action, they form the bedrock of your identity and guide you through life. When your life is in alignment with your values you experience a sense of harmony and purpose. The search for discovering your values is a personal and introspective journey, it requires you to look beyond societal expectations, cultural norms and the desires of others. Your true values are often hidden beneath these layers waiting to be discovered and embraced, it's important to delve deeper to find your true values that you may not have seen before. Have you ever thought about your values, the principles and beliefs that define who you are at your core? They're more than just ethical guidelines, they're what gives meaning to your life. For instance, you might value integrity and always try to act honestly or morally, or maybe compassion is more important to you and you strive to show empathy and concern for others.

Alternatively, you might value creativity and drive to be inactive and original in everything you do. Ultimately your values are what guide you through life and help you make decisions that align with your deepest beliefs. Understanding and acknowledging your values is crucial; they not only define you, but also guide your interactions with the world and when we live in harmony with our values we live a life of authenticity and fulfilment. Reflect on moments in your life when you felt truly happy fulfilled or proud, what were you doing, and what values were you leaning into during these moments? Also, think about moments of frustration and discomfort, often these feelings arrive when your actions are not aligned with your core values. Understanding this conflict can be a powerful tool in helping to identify what truly matters to you. Your values are your internal compass, they guide your decisions and actions, when faced with challenges, it's your values that will illuminate the path that is synchronised with your true self.

Conflicting values

Managing values both internally and with what the world expects from you can be challenging, there may be times when what you value deeply is at odds with what others expect of you and what you have been conditioned to believe. In such scenarios, it's important to reflect and weigh up the importance of each value. Sometimes this may mean making tough choices or even re-evaluating and adjusting your values as you grow and evolve. Integrating your values into your daily life is the key to living authentically. This means making choices - big and small, that are in alignment with your values. It is about being mindful and intentional in your actions ensuring that they reflect your true beliefs. Living your values is an ongoing process, as you grow and change so too will your values, regularly reflecting on and affirming your values is an essential part of staying true to yourself.

The path to your true self through the lenses of your values is not just about finding you - it's about celebrating a life that is authentically and uniquely yours. In a world that often pushes you towards compliance your values stand as inspirations of your individuality, guiding you towards a life of purpose and authenticity.

(Source: positivepsychology.com)

Using the PERMA approach can offer you some fantastic insights into the different areas of your having a structured approach to the idea of happiness and well-being can help you feel a sense of achievement. Although PERMA is only part of a larger positive psychology puzzle, it can be a fantastic starting point for anyone looking to achieve a greater sense of happiness and well-being. For anyone feeling overwhelmed with different areas of their life, this is a good framework to help you feel in control.

21
Setting and pursuing value-based goals

Now that you've pinpointed your core values with the exercises from the book companion at gericarey.com, it's time to set goals that aren't just goals but are true to your values. This is how you ensure every step you take is charged with purpose and passion. Value-based goals are deeply rooted in what truly matters to you, ensuring that your pursuits are aligned with your authentic self and not just driven by external expectations or societal norms.

Understanding value-based goals

Aligned with core values - Value-based goals are those that resonate with your core values. They are not just about achieving a result but about embodying and living according to what you hold most dear.

Fulfilment over achievement - These goals prioritise personal fulfilment over conventional achievements. They are about finding meaning and satisfaction in the pursuit and realisation of the goals.

Holistic approach - Value-based goals consider the whole person; your emotional, mental, and sometimes spiritual well-being, not just the external markers of success.

How to set value-based goals

In today's fast-paced world setting goals is a common practice, however, you can often forget the importance of aligning your goals with your values. Value-based goal setting is a powerful approach that helps you set goals that resonate with your core beliefs and priorities, leading to a more fulfilling and purpose-driven life.

Reflect on your values

Start by revisiting the core values you've identified. Understand how these values manifest in your life and what actions or changes align with them.

Follow a method

Use SMART to make your goals specific and actionable.

For example, if one of your values is 'health', a specific goal could be to engage in physical activity for thirty minutes a day, rather than a vague goal like 'get fit'. You can also use the HEALS CRISPS method which I highly recommend and is shared with you in the next chapter.

Short-term and long-term goals

Set both short-term and long-term goals. Short-term goals can be steps towards your larger, long-term aspirations. For example, if a long-term goal is to write a book (valuing creativity and expression), a short-term goal might be to write a certain number of words each day.

Balance and flexibility

Ensure your goals are balanced and maintain flexibility. Life is dynamic, and your goals should adapt to changes in your circumstances or insights.

Pursuing value-based goals

Chasing goals that resonate with your core values isn't just about getting things done; it's about crafting a life that echoes personal truth and authenticity. Think of these goals as the parts that connect who you are now with who you're striving to become. It is this ongoing process of alignment that brings your values to life, making them a lived experience, not just ideals on paper.

Mindfulness and reflection

Regularly practise mindfulness and reflect on your journey towards these goals. Are your actions still aligned with your values? How do these pursuits make you feel?

Adapt and evolve

Be open to revising your goals as you grow and as your understanding of your values deepens. Life is a journey of evolution, and so are your goals.

Seek support and community

Share your goals with supportive friends or family or find a community with similar values. This support can be invaluable in maintaining motivation and perspective.

Celebrate milestones

Celebrate milestones along the way, not just the achievement of the final goal. Recognise the value in the process and the growth it brings.

Questions to find Values:

Use the following questions to identify the values you hold dearly, consider whether your daily actions align with them and reflect on how much time you get to spend on each one.

- How would you like others to describe you?
- What do you feel gives your life meaning and purpose?
- What makes you feel energised?
- What do you think is worth aspiring for?
- What makes you happiest and most fulfilled?
- What do you want to do?
- What do you want to do?
- How do you want to do it?

What are the values within these areas of your life?

Example:

- Relationship with a partner - trust
- Parenting - caring

- Friends - integrity
- Education - knowledge
- Physical self-care - inner peace

What are your values in everyday life?

Can you list examples? Write about how these values appear in your everyday life.

Looking at how these values appear in your everyday life may give you a clue into any feelings of disconnection that you are experiencing at this moment. You may uncover that you can experience things that are in line with your values and have identified them. Or you may have noticed that you're not able to do many of the things that allow you to make sure your values are acknowledged. For example, if you value connection and you are missing out due to being busy, this will have an impact on you. You may feel tension if you value inner peace and you're not getting time to do the activity that brings you flow or helps you switch off.

Using the HEALS CRISPS Method to set your goals

Many experts suggest using the SMART approach to help achieve your goals: Specific, Measurable, Assignable, Realistic, and Time-bound. However, the concept of SMART goals mostly comes from the perspective of maximising profit and productivity. While SMART goals may help you achieve performance targets, they may not be the best way to enhance your well-being or overcome psychological distress. For instance, buying a new car might be a SMART goal, but remember research indicates that achieving such "extrinsic" goals is not necessarily associated with greater happiness.

Mick Cooper developed the HEALS CRISPS Method, which I've found to be a great alternative to SMART.

Higher-order

Set realistic goals that relate to your fundamental values and link them to a higher purpose.

Effective

Your goals should be meaningful and effective in achieving highest-order wants and needs.

Approach

Positive goals are better than negative ones. You should reframe avoidant goals and focus on increasing healthy, positive emotions.

Longer-term

Prioritise achievable, balanced goals to overcome obstacles and achieve success.

Synergetic

Goals should not conflict with each other. Be aware of 'rogue goals.' you should aim for a balance of goals, pursuing multiple objectives through various strategies.

Challenging

Challenging goals lead to more progress. Encourage yourself to aim higher.

Realistic

It is important to set realistic and achievable goals. If goals are dependent on external factors, they should be reframed. Additionally, it's important to pay attention to the number of goals set, as having too many can be overwhelming. If goals are unattainable, it may be necessary to be flexible and review them.

Intrinsic

Focus on your own goals that align with your intrinsic values. This makes you committed and helps you take ownership.

'Small steps'

Set smaller sub-goals to help achieve realistic objectives. This can boost your self-efficacy and relieve pressure.

Process-focused

It is better to set long-term goals instead of one-time goals to reduce pressure and create a more ongoing sense of well-being. Rather than focusing on explicit goals and sub-goals, it's better to aim for continual self-improvement. View life and plans as an ongoing process, rather than a task to be completed.

Specific

Specific goals are preferred over vague ones because they are easier to measure. However, goals should not be too specific, as they can limit flexibility. It is important to find a balance between specificity and overall importance.

Navigating rogue goals - spot the trouble makers

I love teaching about rogue goals! It's when I see a lot of light bulbs ping as people start to realise that their goals are not their own! You set goals and chase dreams, but are they yours? Those goals that feel like you're wearing someone else's clothes - they might fit, but they don't feel right - are 'rogue goals' and they're more common than you think.

We live in a loud world filled with opinions, expectations, and a constant barrage of ideas about what success looks like. It is easy to get caught up and start chasing things because that's what you're 'supposed' to do. After all, that's what everyone else is doing. Not all goals lead to fulfilment. Some lead you down a path that's not meant for you, leaving you feeling empty, even when you've ticked all the boxes. It is not just about identifying these misleading goals, it's about finding what your way back to the goals that resonate with you, who you truly are, not what the world tells you to be. No sugar-coating, no excuses. This exercise is about taking each of your goals and putting them under the microscope.

Let's run them through the goals filter!

This is about cutting the fluff and getting down to what matters. You might find that some of your goals are perfectly aligned with your true self, and that's great - hold onto those. But if you find rogues, be ready to let them go. It is about quality not quantity, about pursuing goals that resonate with your core, that make you feel alive. Question each goal, analyse its origin and its purpose, this is about taking control of your narrative steering your life in a direction that's authentic to you.

Remember every goal you set shapes your path, so choose the ones that lead you to a life you're excited to live.

T - Test for alignment: Check if the goal aligns with your core values and long-term vision.

R - Relevance: Ensure the goal is relevant to your current life circumstances and direction.

U - Understand motivations: Be clear about why you want to achieve this goal and what it represents for you.

E - Evaluate commitment: Assess your commitment level. Is this a goal you are prepared to work towards consistently?

G - Gauge passion: Measure your passion for the goal. Is it something that excites and motivates you?

O - Obstacles anticipation: Identify potential obstacles and decide if the goal is still attainable, considering these challenges.

A - Assess impact: Consider the potential impact on your life and the lives of others.

L - Long-term perspective: Think about how this goal fits into your long-term objectives.

S - Set criteria for success: Define what success looks like for this goal and how you will measure it.

Using "TRUE GOALS" as your filter, you can thoroughly evaluate each of your goals to determine if they're in line with what's genuinely important to you, ensuring that you're not pursuing 'rogue' goals that don't serve your ultimate purpose.

Can you see the goal? Close your eyes and picture yourself having achieved one of your goals and see in vivid detail - the success, the accomplishment, the lifestyle. Immerse yourself in the scene now and pay close attention to how you feel in this visualisation.

Can you feel the goal? Do you feel like you've come home and are exactly where you're meant to be? Or is there a sense of emptiness, a feeling that something's off?

If your visualisation makes you feel warm, fuzzy and determined like you're fulfilling your mission then you're on the right track. That sense of rightness is exactly what you're aiming for. That is a sign of a goal that's not just a destination but a journey that aligns with your true self. Remember the goal isn't to just succeed in the result, it's to succeed in a way that's meaningful to you.

22

Practising mindfulness: tuning into your inner voice

There's a lot of talk about mindfulness and there's a good reason for it, it works! But what is it? It can be confusing with so much advice out there, but one thing I do know is that it's all about you. You may already have an idea of the benefits from practising mindfulness or perhaps the word is enough to make you cautious. Let us have a look and see if it's something you can include as part of your new routine. Mindfulness is a powerful tool in the journey of self-discovery. It involves being fully present in the moment and being able to observe your thoughts, feelings, and sensations without judgement. By including mindfulness in your life you open the door to a deeper understanding of your inner self.

Research has shown that mindfulness is more than a relaxation technique, it can encourage you to act authentically in line with your values!

Why mindfulness matters

Mindfulness creates an increased awareness of your thoughts and feelings. This heightened awareness helps you understand your reactions and emotions.

Connecting with the present

In our fast-paced world, it's easy to get lost in the hustle and bustle, overlooking what truly matters. Mindfulness brings you back to the present, helping you focus on what is truly important in the here and now.

Reducing stress and anxiety

Regular mindfulness practice can reduce stress and anxiety, creating mental clarity. This clarity allows you to better understand your values and what brings you genuine happiness and fulfilment.

Cultivating inner peace

Mindfulness leads to a sense of inner peace and calm, creating a conducive environment for introspection and self-discovery.

I'm in: how do I do it?

Mindfulness is available to you in every moment, whether through meditations and body scans, or mindful moment practices like taking time to pause and breathe.

Mindfulness practices to discover your values

Mindful breathing

Start with a simple mindful breathing exercise. Focus on your breath, noticing the sensations of inhaling and exhaling. When your mind wanders, gently bring your attention back to your breath. This practice can help centre your thoughts and clear your mind.

Body scan meditation

Engage in a body scan meditation, where you focus on each part of your body in turn, observing any sensations, thoughts, or emotions that arise. This practice can help you become more attuned to your physical and emotional states, deepening your self-awareness.

Mindful observation

Spend time in nature or a quiet space, observing your surroundings with full attention. Notice the sights, sounds, and smells. This practice can help you connect with your sensory experiences and be present in the moment.

Mindful journaling

Combine mindfulness with journaling. After a mindfulness session, write down your thoughts and feelings. Reflect on how these insights relate to your values and desires.

Mindful listening

Practise mindful listening in your interactions with others. Listen intently, without judgement or planning your response. This can enhance your empathy and understanding.

Mindful walking

Try mindful walking, where you focus on the experience of walking, the rhythm of your steps, and the sensations in your body. Use this time to reflect inwardly on what matters most to you.

Integrating mindfulness into daily life

To truly benefit from mindfulness, make it a regular practice. Dedicate time each day to mindfulness exercises. Remember, the goal is not to empty your mind but to observe it. Over time, you'll notice an increased awareness.

23
Self-Led Life® review and appraisal

Forget waiting for a manager or HR; you are self-led now. This means you now review your own performance and goals, you even get to give yourself a score or a bonus, good for you!

You should know by now, there's brilliant printable resources for you to use with space in the book companion visit gericarey.com for all of the information.

Being self-led means, you set up a regular review of your diary and your goals - a personal board meeting with yourself. It is all well and good setting the goals and planning strategy but if you don't take time to look at the progress then how will you learn? Making time to oversee your actions will help make sure you're on track and haven't drifted off course. I take one day once a month to have a Self-Leadership Meeting where I check in with myself and I encourage you to do the same. These meetings are unique, they are a space to explore personal strategy with yourself, for yourself. If you feel you would like some accountability ask someone from your growth circle, to be a coach or look at my website for ways to work with me.

Agenda - me, me and more me

YOUR SL Check-In

Set up a monthly or quarterly review – whatever works for you but stick to it. Make it as important as any key meeting in your life because, frankly, what's more important than the direction of your life? During these check-ins, you're going to do a deep dive into each of your goals and values and capture learnings. Ask yourself: 'Is this goal still serving me? Is it bringing me closer to my authentic self? Or is it a remnant of who I thought I should be?'

This is where you sit down, roll up your sleeves and get real about your progress and direction. This is about making the time for yourself to check in on everything you are putting into place. Set up a monthly or quarterly review - whatever works for you but you need to stick to it. Make it as important as any key meeting in your life because frankly what's more important than the direction you are heading?

During your SL check-in, check each of your goals asking yourself is this still relevant? Is it bringing me closer or is it a rogue goal, something based on who I thought I should be? Be harsh in your evaluation if a goal isn't cutting it if, it's not making you feel engaged alive and true to yourself then it's time to pivot. It is about being agile, being willing to let go of what's not working and having the courage to pursue what does. Remember as you grow and evolve so should your goals, they should be a reflection of your current self, not a shadow of your past.

Don't just stop at evaluating your goals. Look at your actions too. Are they aligning with your goals? It is easy to set a goal, the real work is in the steps you take to achieve it. Are you making progress, however small? Are your actions reflecting your commitment to these goals? If not, it's time to reassess your approach.

How is your growth circle?

Have you found any opportunities for learning? Have you identified a need to work on boundaries etc? Have you noticed any triggers? How does your self-care plan need to be revisited? How is the work/life balance?

What glimmers have you had?

Have you had any glimmers? Have they told you anything? Any patterns yet?

What learning opportunities have arisen?

Have you noticed any areas for deeper learning? Any strong reactions? Triggers?

How can you pass it forward?

Are you seeing the benefits of a Self-Led Life®. Can you create the tidal wave and help others to become the experts in themselves?

Your SL check-in is your tool to stay on track, to ensure that you're not just moving, but moving in the right direction. It ss a tool to keep you honest, focused, and aligned with your true self. So, take it seriously, schedule those reviews, and approach them with the same intensity and honesty you've used throughout this entire process. **Your future self will thank you for it.**

24
What is YOUR mission?

As we enter the final part of the book, I hope that you have a jam-packed companion with all of your insights and you are clear on who YOU are, now it's time to put together your mission statement. You have a voice, a presence, a unique impact that no one else can duplicate. This isn't just a set of fancy words strung together; it will help you capture the essence of your identity, your beliefs, and the profound impact you are destined to make. It speaks of who you are at your core and how you intend to leave your mark on the world.

Your statement will help guide you, reminding you of your path when challenges arise. This is about clarity. It's about knowing your purpose, and that your actions are aligned with your deepest beliefs.

Reflecting on self-identity

Let us revisit the core of who you are, using all of the data you have created and consider the below questions which will guide you into creating your impact statement.

Personal values and beliefs

Some values might be love, freedom, creativity, kindness, adventure, loyalty etc. Your mission statement needs to reflect these values so that you don't end up pursuing a goal in ways that are not a good fit for your values. In addition to your values, include those value-based goals that have been through your goals filter.

- What are those non-negotiable values that you stand by, no matter what?
- Remember these values are your north star, guiding every decision you make, and every step you take.
- Think about the beliefs you now hold about the world.

Strengths and skills

- Recognise what you bring to the table. What are those abilities you have recognised that come naturally to you? Maybe it's your ability to connect with people, your knack for solving complex problems, or perhaps the unique way you see the world. These strengths are your superpowers.

Life experiences

- Recall the peaks, the struggles, the triumphs, and the setbacks – they've all played a part in shaping you. How have they moulded your perspective on life?

This process of reflection is not just about self-awareness; it's the first step in declaring to yourself the unique impact you are meant to have.

The most authentic and powerful impact statement comes from a deep understanding of yourself. Take your time, be honest, and be bold. You're not just scratching the surface; you're excavating the depths of your being to reveal the truest version of yourself.

Bring it together

It is time to bring everything together – your values, your strengths, your experiences – into a statement that resonates with the very core of your being. This is where you articulate your essence and your aspirations in a sentence that is as powerful as a battle cry and as personal as your signature.

The structure

- Start with 'I am...' This is your foundation, your unshakable core. Fill it with your values, your strengths, and your unique essence. 'I am a catalyst for change,' 'I am a beacon of hope,' 'I am an unwavering pillar of strength.' Feel the power in those words. Believe in them because they are your truth.
- Then, transition to 'I aspire to...' This is your vision, your mission. What impact do you want to make? How do you want to influence the world, your community, or even just your inner circle? 'I aspire to inspire,' 'I aspire to challenge the status quo,' 'I aspire to spread kindness like wildfire.' This isn't just wishful thinking; it's a declaration of your path forward.

Short and clear

Keep it short. Keep it clear. This isn't a time for long-winded explanations or flowery prose. This is about getting to the heart of your impact in as few words as possible. A clear, concise statement has the power to stick – in your mind and in the hearts of those who hear it.

Examples for inspiration

I am a relentless seeker of truth and justice, aspiring to bring light to hidden stories.' Or, 'I am a creative soul, aspiring to colour the world with hope and joy.' These are more than just words. They are commitments. They are promises. They are the embodiment of someone's deepest intentions and desires.

Your impact statement is your manifesto. It is a daily reminder of who you are and what you are here to do. It is a tool that keeps you aligned with your purpose, no matter how many obstacles you encounter along your path. So, take a deep breath, look inward, and start writing. This is your moment to claim your space in the world, to stand tall and say, 'This is who I am, and this is the impact I will make. Go on, the world is waiting for the impact of your true self, the person you were always meant to be.

YOUR way of being

Thank you for reading this book and having the courage to expand your awareness and discover who you really are. I hope the journey has filled you with new insights and practical ways to start living as your true self. As you embark on a Self-Led Life® I hope you will continue to practise self-care and compassion because shining a light on yourself can be tiring work. I am excited to see where your new awareness takes you and I hope you continue to make time to explore your inside world and relentlessly remain curious about yourself as your way of being. I hope this helps you to break cycles and become unapologetic in valuing your place on this earth. I hope you now have found the strength, awareness and self-compassion to always be in control of who you think you are and encourage others to do the same. I'd love to know if you found your owl or that loud voice inside that has your back, you do know it has been with you all along, don't you?

Ready to Learn More?

Self-Led Life Training® isn't just any course—it's your gateway to mastering the art of self-direction. Designed to echo the transformative insights of the book, this online course will equip you with the awareness to take charge of your life. It's perfect if you're looking to dive deep into personal growth with all the convenience of learning from home. And don't worry, I'll be right there with you, cheering you on every step of the way, ensuring you're never alone in this journey to unlock your true potential.

Seeking Personalised Support?

If you're looking for dedicated one-on-one guidance to navigate life's challenges, I'm here to help. Whether you need focused therapy, coaching, or a blend of both, I offer tailored support designed to meet your unique needs. Let's take the first step towards understanding and addressing your concerns. Book a discovery call through my website, and together we can explore the best path forward.

If this journey has sparked your interest and you're eager to take the next step, why not head over to my website? Dive deeper into our specialised training options designed for every stage of your personal and professional development. Whether you're looking for 1-to-1 coaching and therapy sessions, or you want to extend your learning with our Self-Led Leader® Training, there's a path tailored just for you.

Want to be a Self-Led Leader?

Research shows that authentic leadership is linked to higher job satisfaction, greater employee engagement, and improved financial performance. Embrace these benefits with our "Self-Led Leader®" course. As a seasoned therapist and coach with over twenty years of expertise in recruitment, HR, and talent management, I bring a wealth of knowledge to the forefront of authentic leadership. This course is not just about imparting knowledge; it's a transformative journey into the heart of your business, empowering both owners and senior leaders to embody the ethos of a Self-Led Leader®.

My Signature Coaching Approach is designed to equip businesses with innovative strategies that place individuals at the core of every decision, ensuring outstanding results and a true win-win situation. Cultivating self-direction within a business isn't solely about boosting efficiency; it's about fostering a dynamic and progressive environment where employees thrive as architects of their own success, aligning their personal growth with the organisation's overarching goals.

Ready to transform your business and lead with authenticity?

Visit **gericarey.com** to learn more about the Self-Led Leader® course and level up with effective authentic leadership.

Bibliography

Berne, E. (2010). *Games people play*. Puffin.

Bernstein, G. (2018). *Judgment detox: Release the beliefs that hold you back from living a better life*. North Star Way.

Brown, B. (2012). *Daring greatly: How the courage to be vulnerable transforms the way we live, Love, parent, and lead*. Baker & Taylor.

Brown, C. (2015). *Understanding person-centred counselling: A personal journey*. Sage.

Cooper, M. (2020, October 3). *Smart goals for counselling and psychotherapy? try healing crisps*. Mick Cooper Training and Consultancy. https://mick-cooper.squarespace.com/new-blog/2020/6/17/smart-goals-for-counselling-and-psychotherapy-youre-better-off-healing-crisps#:~:text=Unfortunately%2C%20after%20many%20hours%20on,Sorry!

Csikszentmihalyi, M. (2016). *Flow and the foundations of positive psychology: The collected works of mihaly csikszentmihalyi*. Springer.

Frankl, V. E., Kushner, H. S., & Winslade, W. J. (2006). *Man's search for meaning*. Beacon Press.

Harris, R. (2012). *The happiness trap: Based on act - A revolutionary mindfulness-based programme for overcoming stress, anxiety and depression*. Robinson.

Kolk, B. V. D. (2022). *Body keeps the score*. VIVAT.

Moustakas, C. E. (2013). *Heuristic research: Design, methodology, and applications*. Sage Publications.

Neff, K. (2021). *Fierce self-compassion how women can harness kindness to speak up, claim their power, and thrive*. HarperCollins Publishers.

P., S. M. E. (2018). *Learned optimism: How to change your mind and your life*. Nicholas Brealey.

Rogers, C. R. (1995). *A way of being*. Houghton Mifflin.

Rogers, C. R. (2004). *On becoming a person: A therapist's view of psychotherapy*. Constable.

Rotter, J. B. (1954). *Social Learning and Clinical Psychology.* https://doi.org/10.1037/10788-000

Schwartz, R. C. (2023). *No bad parts: Healing trauma & restoring wholeness*. Vermilion.

Seligman, M. (2011). *Flourish*. Nicholas Brealey.

Sultan, N. (2019). *Heuristic inquiry: Researching human experience holistically*. SAGE Publications, Inc.

About the Author

Geri is an accredited Psychotherapist, business owner and coach. In addition to her interest in Psychology and Psychotherapy, Geri has always been passionate about all things related to human potential.

She holds a master's degree in Psychotherapy and Counselling from Keele University, a graduate certificate in Psychotherapy and Counselling, and a postgraduate diploma in Positive Psychology.

Geri has seen time and again that getting to know and accept who we are leads directly to a clearer, more confident outlook. This self-recognition and acceptance is what can truly help you improve your life.

Geri has created way to help you take back control of your own life, the Self-Led Life® isn't just about knowing who you are, its about understanding the forces that have shaped you and using that knowledge to create a better life.

Ways to connect with Geri:

- Individual Coaching & Therapy sessions.
- Self-Led Leader® Training
- Person-Centred Transformational Coaching for therapists and coaches
- Geri carey.com for the weekly newsletter and Who the F*ck do you THINK you are Podcast

Connect with Geri to help you uncover your path to personal leadership. Schedule a discovery call via gericarey.com.